GdB Business Sc

Operational Risk and Resilience

Operational Risk and Resilience

Chris Frost, David Allen, James Porter and Philip Bloodworth

OXFORD AUCKLAND BOSTON JOHANNESBURG MELBOURNE NEW DELHI

Butterworth-Heinemann
Linacre House, Jordan Hill, Oxford OX2 8DP
225 Wildwood Avenue, Woburn, MA 01801-2041
A division of Reed Educational and Professional Publishing Ltd

℞ A member of the Reed Elsevier plc group

First published 2001

© PricewaterhouseCoopers 2001

British Library Cataloguing in Publication Data
A catalogue record for this book is available from the British Library

Library of Congress Cataloguing in Publication Data
A catalogue record for this book is available from the Library of Congress

ISBN 0 7506 4395 1

Typeset by Avocet Typeset, Brill, Aylesbury, Bucks
Printed and bound in Great Britain by Biddles Ltd, *www.biddles.co.uk*

FOR EVERY TITLE THAT WE PUBLISH, BUTTERWORTH-HEINEMANN
WILL PAY FOR BTCV TO PLANT AND CARE FOR A TREE.

Contents

Foreword

This book is about 'rethinking' traditional ideas and practices in the area of operational risk management. It is also about 'rethinking' the nature of risk, risk management, and operations management in general. Its aim is to raise awareness of a relatively new area of management focus – operational risk management – and offer practical solutions that will help managers walk the fine line between success and failure as we move into the twenty-first century.

In the 1980s and 1990s, much of the focus in risk management circles revolved around designing and implementing control frameworks, managing insurance portfolios and meeting corporate governance standards following the increased attention focused on corporate governance and the publication of the Greenbury, Cadbury and later the Hampel reports.

In certain industries, a great deal of attention has been given to the identification and elimination of risk. In the nuclear sector, for example, the consequences of failure were known to be so catastrophic that the prospect of failure was seen to be unacceptable. As a result, risk management experts in the industry developed new approaches to the quantification of risk, but often in narrowly focused areas that were not directly relevant elsewhere. In the financial sector, considerable attention has been placed on the management of credit and market risk. Across global financial markets, complex mathematical models are used to calculate the extent of potential risk exposures.

As the pace of change continues to accelerate, many organizations are now finding that they can no longer afford to take a solely defensive attitude to risk. While control frameworks are a necessary first step in managing risk, many organizations now need to manage risk for strategic advantage, to improve customer satisfaction and increase share-holder value. In the trading rooms around the world, one of the primary goals of risk management is to guide the process of risk-taking by traders.

The aim of operational risk management is to help organizations achieve their strategic goals. By its nature, operational risk management is the integration of risk management with core operations manage-ment. As well as offering a structure for designing and implementing controls that support business objectives, operational risk management can also help ensure that organizations deliver shareholder value. Risk management and corporate strategy are becoming more closely aligned than ever before.

The aim of this book is to help managers achieve two objectives:

- to implement (an appropriate) control structure aligned with busi-ness objectives; and

- to use operational risk management as a tool to improve service delivery.

In Chapter 1, the authors introduce the subject of operational risk man-agement and examine why it is seen as an area for attention today. In particular, they examine the wider business context in which effective operational risk management is becoming paramount for many organ-izations today.

Chapter 2 examines different ways of establishing operational risk frameworks designed to help managers achieve operational integrity. Following the increasing pressure from regulators for management to focus on risks and control (e.g. the recent Turnbull Report published in the UK, as discussed in Chapter 4), this has become even more of a pri-ority for organizations. In other countries, similar corporate governance initiatives have put organizations under pressure to implement more structured risk management frameworks.

In Chapter 3, we examine how organizations can use operational risk management to improve the delivery of their products and services to the market, as well as the chances of success of new projects. We show that by building 'resilience' in operations, organizations can better deliver their product or service to their customers, increase customer satisfaction and ultimately, increase shareholder value.

Finally, Chapter 4 takes a look at aspects of the management of operational risk that are becoming increasingly important as we move into the twenty-first century:

- operational risk management in the financial sector; and

- how organizations can increase their chances of success in new business areas, such as electronic business.

There is no 'one size fits all' solution, however. Although managers across industry sectors face many common goals from needing to improve customer satisfaction to the need to generate shareholder value, we know that organizations in different sectors face different risks. The authors of this book have set out to describe a number of approaches to this end. The challenge for all of us is to learn from the past and to use that knowledge to build the future.

References

Cadbury Report: Report of the Committee on the Financial Aspects of Corporate Governance, Gee Publishing Ltd, 1 December 1992.
Greenbury Report: Directors' Remuneration – A Report of a Study Chaired by Sir Richard Greenbury, Gee Publishing Ltd, July 1995.
Hampel Report: The Committee on Corporate Governance, Gee Publishing Ltd, January 1998.

Jeff Thompson
Partner, PricewaterhouseCoopers Global Leader
Operational Risk Services

Acknowledgements

This book is based on a combination of several research projects and extensive practical experience gained in industry.

Our special thanks go to the many PricewaterhouseCoopers professionals who provided their support and energy. We are particularly grateful to the individuals who collaborated by sharing their ideas, experience and research results: Dave Allen, Richard Anderson, Geoff Campbell, James Chrispin, Sean Cunningham, George Gilmour, Andrew Gray, Paul Jacob, Charles Johnson, Bernard Kenny, Neil Osborne, Sam Samaratunga, Stephen Sloan, Steve Stocks and Graham Ward.

The authors would particularly like to thank Geoff Smart for his significant contribution to the project risk management section and Dr Paul Wilhelmij and colleagues for their permission to cite their work on the Lifetrack Project.

We must also thank our editor, Ben Hunt, for his patience and for his help in bringing together the many parts of this book.

Risk
management overview

Introduction to operational risk management

At a macro-level, a country's economy is dependent on processes in government, industrial, service and infrastructure sectors running smoothly and efficiently. When they do not – for example, as a result of natural disaster, industrial action or a major financial crisis – an economic price is paid in terms of lost competitiveness, increased running costs, lower future growth expectations, unemployment or even recession.

At a micro-economic level, individual organizations also face the risk that their activities and processes may be disrupted unexpectedly or fail to meet expected performance levels. Recent high profile failures – Barings, Piper Alpha and Exxon Valdez – have focused attention at every level on the importance of risk management. The consequences of failures and disruption on performance may be more or less severe – running from minor losses arising from processing backlogs, reduced customer service quality, loss of reputation, and in the extreme, to bankruptcy.

What is clear at a boardroom level is that strong risk management is an essential part of good corporate governance and something that helps to protect shareholder value. There is also a growing recognition of the need to ensure that an effective framework of management controls and supervision is in place. This view is reflected in the attention that is being placed on risk management by regulators and listing authorities around the world.

The aim of operational risk management – the subject of this book – is to ensure that the varied exposures to operational risk faced by an organization are identified and addressed in the most efficient way possible. The achievement of this goal is dependent on management taking positive actions to consider what steps should be taken to optimize an organization's exposure to operational risk so that shareholder value gains can be maximized.

The scope of operational risk management at the highest level can be broken down into two main components:

- operational integrity – the adequacy of operational controls and corporate governance; and

- service delivery – the organization's ability to perform business processes on an ongoing basis.

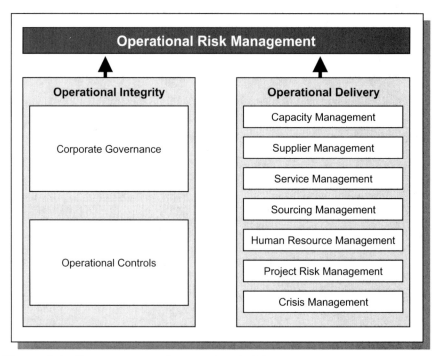

Figure 1.1 Components of operational risk management

There may be many interdependencies between these two core components – for example, a derivatives loss in a bank caused by illegal trading in an environment with poor operational controls may also be the result of poor human resource management.

They may also be considered separately. Operational integrity generally encompasses the management of operational risks stemming from inappropriate cultural environments, lack of management supervision, errors, malice, fraud, poor health and safety and environmental compliance failures, physical disasters, and poor internal controls. Operational delivery covers the management of risks in unexpected sources in demand business operations, processes, failed projects change, supplier relationships, delivery, personnel, IT, premises and plant, and crises.

The evolution of risk management

Traditionally, there have been two strands to corporate risk management: financial and insurance. These risks are managed in different parts of an organization: insurance matters are dealt with by the insurance or risk manager, while the corporate treasurer or finance director has responsibility for financial risk management.

Over the years, risk management has had to evolve with the times. In the 1970s, risk managers started to pay more attention to active risk control and risk management started to become more proactive than in the past. On the financial side, they saw a need to hedge against increasing economic volatility in the shape of fluctuating currency and commodity values. New financial derivatives markets were born, and the discipline of financial risk management took off in corporate treasury departments and banks around the world.

In the 1980s, enterprises became more sensitized to political and country risk. In 1979, US businesses lost an estimated $1bn as a result of the Iranian revolution and the overthrow of the Shah. There was a need to analyse the risks of investing in countries, and for banks, the credit risk involved with lending to new borrowers.

In the late 1980s and early 1990s the impact of major fluctuations in the global financial market led to the establishment of market risk management functions in the larger financial institutions.

As the millennium neared, risk management has risen up the corporate agenda and has become a priority for organizations in a wide range of sectors. It has managed to shrug off its main function as a cost-cutting exercise. Increasingly, boards are realizing that it has strategic importance. The fact that some sophisticated financial institutions now have chief risk officers (CROs) sitting on their boards is testimony to this.

In today's rapidly changing business climate there is a need for a fresh approach to risk management. In particular, boards need to focus more on managing risk for strategic advantage. This is where synergies between traditional risk management practices and operations management have fallen down in the past. Risk management has often been too defensive, focusing mainly on hazard risk rather than the upside potential involved with positive risk-taking.

While management at an operational level often focuses on the smooth and efficient running of an organization, attention is not always given to management of operational risk within the context of an enterprise-wide view of risk. One drawback however, is that it is too often framed at an operational level within organizations. As a result, it remains apart from strategic considerations. One of the main messages of this book is that in today's world, organizations need to focus on an approach to risk management that is aligned with forward-looking growth strategies for achieving competitive advantage. This approach should go hand in hand with maintaining 'operational resilience' – the ability to handle operational stress. Overall, organizations that achieve greater stability have a better foundation to compete more competently in the market and provide high service levels to their customers.

A typical operational risk management programme focused on both helping an organization meet operational integrity and delivery objectives is likely to encompass a wide range of activities including:

- defining the scope of operational risk management (alongside other risk management functions, for example, credit and market risk management);

- defining and putting in place the necessary roles and responsibilities and reporting structures;

- identifying categories of risk, prioritizing them and mapping them against business processes to understand their impact;

- working with businesses to assign ownership for managing each risk;

- assisting businesses to identify and implement the necessary controls; and

- implementing the required measures, methods and tools.

Another fundamental driver is the importance of core business processes at the heart of most organizations that serve as basic enablers for other parts of the business. In many organizations, operations management 'owns' around three-quarters of total

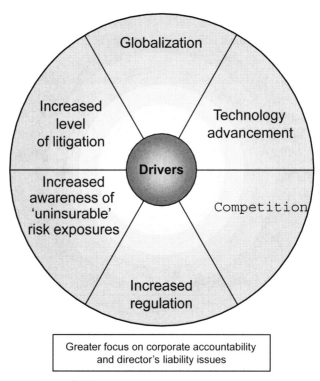

Figure 1.2 Drivers of change

head count, and assets. It is the core process that produces the products and services that generate revenue and accounts for the lion's share of operating costs.

The consequences of not managing operational risk properly go beyond direct financial losses. Failure at the level of operational continuity can lead to what organizations fear most – a loss of reputation among the public at large and their shareholders. In the event of a problem, organizations may find it very difficult to recover damage to market share, brand-value or to regain competitive advantage after an unexpected shock.

Recent high profile failing of Internet start-up businesses have resulted in billions of dollars of market capitalization being wiped out overnight.

An effective way of examining operational risk is by looking at the consequences to the organization of events disrupting specific processes:

- direct financial losses, which arise from failing to meet an obligation (for example, penalty interest payments or restitution costs);

- direct financial losses, attributable to an absence of income (for example, from loss of sales, transaction fees, direct fees or commission);

- statutory or regulatory penalties, ranging from censure to revocation of licences; and

- opportunity costs, arising from adverse publicity, being unable to trade or because of processing delays, backlogs, poor customer service delivery or poor product or service quality.

One of the outputs from an effective operational risk management approach is an operational risk profile (see Figure 1.3) that provides a clear picture of the risks facing an organization.

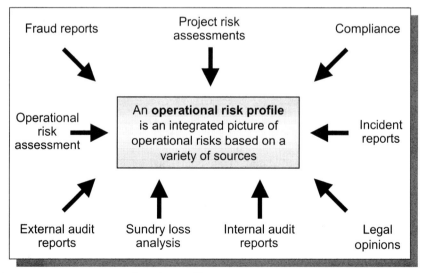

Figure 1.3 Operational risk profile

Why is ORM becoming an issue?

While operational risk management (ORM) practices in some industry sectors are well established – such as in the nuclear power and air transportation industries – the need for a systematic approach to ORM is only now starting to enter into the wider business consciousness. One of the most immediate business drivers for taking operational risk management more seriously now than in the past is demonstrated by those organizations that have suffered catastrophic failure because of poor operational risk management. Barings Bank, which collapsed as a result of the massive losses caused by Nick Leeson and his illegal derivatives trading activities is a high-profile example of this kind of failure.

As we move into the twenty-first century the rate of change is becoming one of the most important issues facing management. Some of the drivers of change that have increased exposure to operational risk for organizations across most industry sectors are outlined below.

Globalization

In today's more competitive economic climate, organizations are finding it less easy to be complacent about their traditional business and organizational strengths. Organizations with traditional manufacturing or supply chain processes are finding it increasingly hard to compete because of pressures on margins and the response to customer expectations. As a result, many are moving away from defensive manoeuvres in search of new ways of gaining a competitive advantage that is sustainable in the longer term. This often entails pursuing rapid growth in new markets or regions, stretching existing management resources and putting greater strain on operational performance.

Growth of e-business

Today, complex and often high-risk operational processes and systems are at the heart of sophisticated 'information age' economies in Europe, the Americas and the Asia Pacific rim. The introduction of new technologies has increased efficiency but has also led to new complex business interdependencies. The explosive growth of e-business in every sector, coupled with the rising use of 'mission-critical' corporate extranets and intranets and the automation of various tasks performed by blue and increasingly white collar workers, are just two examples. Reliance on new technology tends to concentrate risk and increase the impact of operational failure. At a macro-level, there is a risk that whole operations will fail. At a micro-level, the increase in the volume of transactions, and the increase in transaction processing speeds also increases the rate at which errors are processed and their potential impact.

Competition

Both consumer-to-business and business-to-business markets are less tolerant of delay and errors than ever before. They expect high levels of service quality, at low cost and on time. Poor service quality can quickly lead to a loss of market share. This is putting greater pressure on businesses to avoid any discontinuity in service and product delivery.

Increased regulation

Organizations are increasingly faced with new regulations, at the level of health and safety, the environment, competition, customer rights protection, and so on. Many regulatory agencies now adopt a more stringent approach and are more prone to fine organizations for compliance breaches. A greater focus is being put on direction liabilities than in the past, with imprisonment being needed as a punishment in the extreme. This new approach highlights the need for a more sophisticated system of management supervision and control, particularly at the operations level.

Increased awareness of 'uninsurable' risk exposures

Many organizations today, especially if they are large multinationals, have the financial resources to cope with major physical disasters, such as a chemical plant explosion, fire or floods. A number of these organizations are now establishing captive insurance companies as a form of self-insurance. For those organizations that choose to use the insurance industry, there are an increasing number of insurance companies willing to cover such risk exposures. There is also a realization that some of the greatest risks faced by successful organizations are intangible – such as those that could damage their reputation in the marketplace. These risks are potentially more damaging because they directly affect business operations; if a business loses market share, the volume of sales may never recover. A gutted building, by contrast, can be replaced in a matter of weeks. At the same time, the nature of these risks mean that they are harder to find insurance cover for. Increasing awareness of these types of risk has meant operational continuity is more critical.

Increased level of litigation

The world is becoming more litigious and increasingly businesses and consumers are seeking legal redress when things go wrong. The use of the civil courts to seek redress for perceived wrongs has resulted in litigation in areas where it was rarely seen in the past. The rising threat of litigation in the product liability sphere, and relatively new exposures such as those associated with sexual equality, are increasing the chances of costly court cases and damage to reputation.

In the UK, there have been several high-profile court cases involving financial institutions that have been shown to dis-

criminate against female employees and have had to pay significant damages.

Greater focus on corporate accountability and directors' liability issues

Over the course of the 1990s, boardrooms around the world
have been influenced by the corporate governance bandwagon
– the attempt to ensure that companies are run in the interests
of their owners, the shareholders.

At the same time, new legislation has also forced an urgent
reappraisal of enterprise-wide risk management practice. The
changes to corporate manslaughter legislation proposed in the
UK are an example. Boards would be responsible for injury or
death caused to the public through negligence. Since corporate
history is littered with major disasters that have involved the
deaths of members of the public, as well as those of
employees, from the Bhopal accident in India in 1984 to the
Herald of Free Enterprise ferry disaster of 1987, this legislation could be expected to provoke boards to see to it themselves that their organizations have adequate risk management
processes.

Managing public expectations

One factor organizations are having to take into account is the
growing level of public interest in environmental and social
issues. This can have the knock-on effect of consumer action
in form of product or service boycotts.

One example from recent history was the outcry faced by the
board of Shell in the mid-1990s over its decision to use a deep
water disposal strategy for the Brent Spar oil rig. After considerable consumer and, in some cases, government pressure
because of the perceived environmental issues, Shell had to
resort to disposing the platform by other means, but not until

it had lost several million dollars of revenue through consumer action.

Rethinking risk

In many ways, the constantly changing nature of today's global economy is not well suited to the cautious, risk-averse entrepreneur. The need for flexibility and the ability to embrace continuous change has introduced a whole new set of challenges for executives around the world as they come under increasing competitive pressure in the global marketplace. These challenges have reshaped the way in which risk is perceived.

Research has shown that many of the organizations that are successful in the constantly changing business environment place a premium on innovation, risk-taking and entrepreneurship and strive to develop a 'breakthrough' culture – a culture where ongoing experimentation thrives.

The benefits of risk-taking are clear. Progress – economic or otherwise – implies risk-taking of some kind, to mark a break from convention and change for the better. Not only are there tangible rewards at the end of the process that may come from experimentation and the creation of new products, organizations also benefit from the confidence and experience acquired in the process. The US economic environment not only encourages innovative initiatives but also has a business culture that does not stigmatize failure, but instead learns from it.

As organizations continue to need to take risks, risk managers should try to avoid stifling this need by being over-defensive. One very important cost of a risk management approach that focuses on risk elimination when it is not appropriate to do so, is a negative impact on initiative, innovation and entrepreneurship. Excessive emphasis on avoiding failure can ultimately lead to failure, because survival of most businesses is dependent on management taking risks in pursuit of opportunities. Risk-taking is integral to the process of generating shareholder value.

An important point made in this book is that the main rationale for implementing operational risk management should not be to defend an organization against hazard risks. Today, defensive behaviour alone – for example, head count reductions on cost-cutting exercises – cannot lead to the generation of substantial competitive advantage. Boards of companies everywhere are revisiting their values at a strategic level in order to achieve sustainable competitive advantage.

At present, risk management practices in many of the world's largest organizations still tend to be based around a narrow definition of the word 'risk'. In the past, many risk managers were tasked with focusing on managing the downside aspects of risk. Consequently, the focus has often been on managing or controlling hazards – fraudulent behaviour, security breaches, theft, compliance breaches, damage to property, and so on. While these are important, they need to be complemented by an approach that views risk in its upside potential.

Change is on the way. Many recently privatized organizations recognize that their cultures do not encourage the kind of risk-taking needed to maximize shareholder value. They also realize that many of the risks they do take are poorly managed. Moreover, in recent years, executives in a wide range of diverse sectors including oil, biotechnology, mutual funds, consumer products and banking, have launched major initiatives to improve their approach to the management of risk. These initiatives focus on actively managing risks that must be taken in the pursuit of opportunity and, ultimately, profit. This contrasts with the more traditional notion of 'risk management' which involves protecting the organization from losses through control procedures and hedging techniques.

One of the problems faced by risk managers is that the word 'risk' is used in many ways in different fields encompassing competition risk, market risk, financial risk, litigation risk and a plethora of other risks depending on circumstances. A good place to start is to try to rethink the way in which the work 'risk' is used – which was a starting point for a research project involving both PricewaterhouseCoopers and the Harvard Business School.

The Business Risk Continuum™ (BRC) developed by Lee Puschaver (PwC partner) and Professor Robert G. Eccles (Harvard Business School) links the various types of risk and is shown in Figure 1.4.

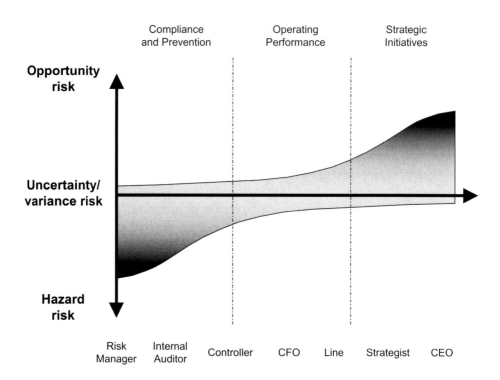

Figure 1.4 Business Risk Continuum™

Managing the upside of risk

Managing the upside of risk in some ways can been seen as an 'offensive' strategy, demanding management decisions designed to exploit opportunities and achieve positive gains. An analysis of upside risk creates insights that can be used by management to increase the probability of success and decrease the probability of failure.

Managing risk on the downside

Managing risk on the downside is often a 'defensive' response and covers the prevention or mitigation of hazards arising from failures, incidents and the actions of employees and others that can generate losses. This approach is based on implementing policies, procedures, controls and systems designed to prevent behaviours that can negatively impact organization performance – including violations of company policies, and external laws and regulations.

Risk analysis technique – the Delphi process

Originally developed at Rand Corporation in the 1950s, the Delphi process is a forecasting technique. It is based on repeated polling of the same experts and the exposure of all participants to evolving group opinions as a basis for later polls. The questionnaire rounds are designed to achieve consensus by allowing the participants to modify their responses in each round in light of the collected responses received in the previous rounds. The process is anonymous; the participants interact only through the published findings of the questionnaire circulated by the Delphi co-ordinator. The intention is to assure that changes in responses reflect rational judgement rather than the influence of high-profile opinion leaders.

The basic premises of the Delphi process are that repeated polling will decrease and converge the range of responses and that the emerging consensus will move toward 'correct' answers. The feedback mechanism, designed to stimulate the participants' thinking, reveals to them factors or developments they might otherwise overlook. Because the participants remain anonymous, they feel more comfortable if and when they change their earlier responses in light of new knowledge or insights accumulated by the process.

A modified Delphi process can be effectively used for the selection of performance measures. Instead of repeated polling, the results of the initial questionnaire survey are organized and discussed in a workshop to arrive at an agreed set of performance measures.

Managing uncertainty

Managing uncertainty is critically important for achieving the best overall performance. Drawing upon hedging techniques, budgets, and other tools, it seeks to ensure that an organization's actual performance meets or exceeds defined goals. Managing uncertainty requires executives to pull together the organization's management systems – from management information through performance measurement to incentive programmes – to establish and achieve the range. As a practical matter, it often also has defensive overtones because it usually trades off some upside gain in order to limit downside losses.

Plotting the different perceptions of risk against the functional areas shows risk as a continuum running through the organization with different emphasis in its different forms.

In some industries, risk-taking is prevalent and encouraged at every level. There is a greater focus on opportunity risks. In many cases, formal risk management procedures are in place. There are two main reasons why this is the case.

First, the extremely dynamic nature of some industry sectors such as entertainment and telecommunications creates great uncertainty and performance pressure. To be successful demands quick action and substantial commitments of resources. Executives now realize that some of the biggest risks they face relate to lost opportunities caused by failure to act quickly and decisively enough.

Second, formal risk management techniques are harder to develop in some sectors. Compared with oil exploration and drug development projects, for example, investment projects are often short-term and elude evaluation on a regular basis. It is therefore hard to conduct risk assessment prior to investment and during development.

The PricewaterhouseCoopers research that led to the development of the BRC went further and compared the BRC of organizations with different goals and objectives. It found that the BRC was different, for example, between an oil exploration organization and a power generator. Equally, the BRC was found to vary between different parts of the same organization.

The BRC also highlights other factors. One of these is that it helps management envision the emphasis they wish to place on managing risk and the resources they want to apply. Moulding and changing these perceptions of risk, and its management, can help organizations to achieve their goals more effectively.

Whilst senior executives have a natural focus towards the upside, boards of directors and executive committees have a responsibility to ensure that all risk across the continuum is managed. This can only occur if risk is understood and reported across all three areas that make up the continuum.

Each of these three elements of risk is connected with one or more functions within the organization. Typically, *hazard* risk is associated with the compliance and prevention functions such as internal audit, financial controllers, as well as insurance and security managers. Risk, as *uncertainty* is the governing perception amongst senior finance officials and line management responsible for sales and commercial operations. Risk as *opportunity* reflects the outlook of senior management and strategies.

From management's perspective, the first step toward clarity is the recognition that each 'risk' issue must be viewed from three distinct perspectives:

- risk as opportunity;

- risk as uncertainty; and

- risk as hazard.

Opportunity

By viewing risk as an opportunity, the inherent relationship between risk and return becomes apparent. The greater the risk, the greater the potential return and, by extension, the greater the potential for loss. Risk may have both qualitative and quantitative aspects. Organizations can use techniques that increase the likelihood of positive returns within the constraints of their operating environments, and risk analysis can also be used to identify opportunities to be exploited. Managing risk as opportunity is an 'offensive' function, necessitating actions being taken by management to achieve positive gains.

Uncertainty

It is also productive to consider the notion of risk as uncertainty. Organizations can determine how they can be proactive in preventing uncertain future events from having a negative impact. The management of uncertainty seeks to ensure that an organization's actual performance falls within a defined range. Uncertainty management can have a strong defensive element, because it may involve the sacrifice of opportunities in order to mitigate losses.

Risk as 'uncertainty' is a more academic use of the word. Here, it refers to the distribution of all possible outcomes, both positive and negative. Risk management in this role seeks to reduce the variance between anticipated outcomes and actual results.

Hazard

Risk can also be viewed as hazard, or a negative event, which may include financial loss, fraud, theft, damage to reputation, injury or death, systems failure, or an unsuccessful legal action. While managing risk as hazard, individuals tend to act in a reactive mode – they mitigate the degree of damage that would be caused should a particular event occur. Individuals who view risks as hazards typically respond in a different way to those viewing the same risks as uncertainties or opportunities.

Risk, as 'hazard' is what managers most mean by the term. They are referring to potential negative events such as financial loss, fraud, a product recall, injury or death in a plant, environmental contamination, or a lawsuit. What all these categories have in common is that they describe the downside element of risk. Managing risk then means installing management techniques to reduce the probability of the negative event without incurring excessive costs or paralysing the organization.

All global companies deal with the three elements of risk management. Which elements they emphasize will depend on the competitive dynamics they face and their strategies. An investment bank takes more risk than an entity in an economy's public sector, for example. In diversified corporations, the relative emphasis can vary substantially across business units and activities.

The following questions may help to clarify the organizational viewpoint:

- Opportunity perspective: Is there any way I can identify opportunities by analysing the risks facing my organization?

- Uncertainty perspective: How can I meet my monthly operational targets?

- Hazard perspective: What is my contingency plan should a negative event actually occur?

If an organization was looking to boost its sales by introducing a new product, as an example, an analysis of the risk issues involved in hiring new sales personnel, using the above framework may result in multiple views of the same issue.

Where risk is viewed as uncertainty, the response may be to establish an advanced sales hiring and training programme. When viewed as hazard, the possibility of failure – the organization may not be able to hire enough sales people – would have to be accepted. A response might be to develop a contingency plan to distribute the new product by other means, such as a joint venture with another organization. Finally, where the risk is viewed as opportunity, it be may be recognized that the potential joint venture partner, identified previously, has access to much broader markets. This may lead to a greater focus on setting up a joint venture agreement.

Having developed this new approach to thinking about the nature of risk in business, PricewaterhouseCoopers realized that there was a need to rethink the way in which risk is managed. The result of this rethinking is the Business Risk Management Framework (BRMF, shown in Figure 1.5).

The BRMF is represented graphically in a four-sided pyramid. The upper levels of the pyramid depict four key aspects of risk management:

- objectives;

Figure 1.5 The Businesses Risk Management Framework

- risks;

- control processes;

- alignment.

These four elements are collectively known as ORCA. ORCA is a conceptual framework developed by Pricewaterhouse-Coopers that rethinks the way in which organizations approach the management of risk. Each element of ORCA takes into account a different aspect of risk management and, taken together, the elements provide a comprehensive and integrated approach to managing risk that can be used as the basis for an organization's risk management vocabulary and philosophy. Finally, complementary ORCA is an enterprise-wide risk management architecture (RMA). This is the second component of BRMF and is represented by the base of the pyramid, symbolizing the relationship between the ORCA principles of risk management and the risk management architecture on which they depend. The architecture constitutes the resources and infrastructure necessary to ensure the consistent application of ORCA; it embodies an eight-point plan for enterprise-wide risk management that includes a common language, leadership, resources, technology, measuring, reporting and organizations.

> '... risk is inherent in business. Although the nature and extent may differ, risk is as applicable to a small retailer as it is to a multinational conglomerate. An organization takes risks in order to pursue opportunities to earn returns for its owners; striking a balance between risk and return is key to maximizing shareholder wealth.'

The development of ORCA as a tool to help organizations develop a risk management capability was an attempt to improve upon the control-focused frameworks in place within many organizations. When applied, the ORCA principles give every individual in an organization a mechanism that leads to a consistent, recurring consideration of risk and reward in day-to-day planning, execution of strategy and achievement of objectives.

One of the key starting points for the development of ORCA was the observation that many of the organizations that have suffered crises in recent years have had highly regarded internal audit, compliance and legal functions, as well as a complex array of control processes. But these control-focused frameworks do not capture the complexity of risk taking and risk management. In particular, control functions that tend to rely heavily on the use of detailed checklists to determine whether appropriate controls are in place struggle to handle the impact of change and tend to employ a 'bottom up' approach. But this 'bottom up' approach can be found wanting on several fronts. Senior management is, typically, not engaged in the process. And checklist-based approaches are often too static, constantly waiting for the next version to be updated following changes to company policy, law, or control models. This tends to mean that some forms of change (typically the more predictable changes such as new tax laws or accounting rules) can be dealt with effectively by these controls. Other forms of change – such as senior management strategic initiatives in response to competitors' actions – however, may expose the existing system and risk management process as inflexible.

One of the key goals of ORCA is to help ensure that management has a clearly defined responsibility for assessing and controlling the risks resulting not only from day-to-day operations, but also from the impact of constant strategic and operational change. To put it more succinctly, responsibility for managing risk should fall with those most responsible for making change. ORCA provides a 'top-down' risk management approach. It captures the new desire among senior managers to view risk from a holistic, or enterprise-wide perspective – a trend that has developed in the last few years. Integration does not just happen of its own accord, however; it is invariably the result of deliberate management strategy.

An additional important point is that the BRMF takes a more integrated view of risk itself. Much work has been done over the last decade on the development of 'control frameworks'. The next stage is to move towards the development of 'business risk management frameworks'. These may be characterized as a form of risk management that realigns the relationship between risk, growth and return to an organization's advantage. The aim of ORCA, therefore, is to help organizations develop a risk management capability that instils, in every individual in the organization, an instinctive, consistent and recurring consideration of risk and reward in the day-to-day planning, execution and achievement of strategic objectives.

This is linked to an appreciation of shareholder value. The BRMF is founded on the premise that risks must be taken in the pursuit of opportunities to increase shareholder value. By aiming to minimize the impact of value-destroying events, and taking into account areas of uncertainty, a key objective is to ensure that organizations achieve greater *consistency* in their financial performance. The main goal is not to eliminate risk, therefore, but rather to be proactive in the assessment and management of risk for strategic advantage.

Level of sophistication in establishing risk management

To explain business risk management more clearly, it may be helpful to describe organizations at different levels of maturity:

- At one end of the spectrum, organizations manage risk in a reactive mode. They only implement new control processes when an unmanaged risk becomes a problem or results in a crisis.

- The next level is where organizations attempt to understand the full extent of the risks facing them. They define risk management as something broader than control over financial processes. They evaluate operational and reputational risks. They search for best-practice processes. When management in these organizations observes a competitor suffering a major control breakdown, it reassesses or revamps its current risk management processes to avoid a similar disintegration.

- More sophisticated organizations understand the relationship between risk and change, and align business objectives with processes that are better equipped to achieve those objectives. This requires an ability to involve operating management in risk evaluation and mitigation processes. Risk management frameworks are used to provide a common language and a consistent approach to risk.

- The next stage involves the incorporation of opportunity into risk evaluation. Organizations evaluate their most sensitive drivers of shareholder value and undertake new strategies and tactics designed to exploit fully those drivers. When appropriate, they change their business objectives to take advantage of identified opportunities. They evaluate their risks on the basis of these new objectives, and build controls and risk management processes into their actions. They strive to turn hazards into opportunities. These companies approach strategic decisions utilizing the latest techniques for maximizing shareholder value. They use risk for decision making and decision monitoring. Risk-adjusted rates of return are used for capital allocation and return evaluation of current businesses and contemplated investments.

- At the top end of the 'risk management continuum' are the organizations that integrate risk management more fully with the goals of achieving superior and sustainable shareholder value. These organizations shift the responsibility for managing risk away from controllers, internal auditors, and compliance officers, to everyone in the organization. They supply their employees with frameworks that focus attention on risk management rather than risk criteria. They make use of comprehensive real-time technology tools to support and facilitate the risk management. They have

> extensive communication and organization-wide train-
> ing programmes to help their employees improve their
> risk management skills.

Some of the benefits of establishing a risk management framework such as the BRMF include:

- gaining an understanding of risk as an opportunity, rather
  than as a threat to be avoided;

- leveraging competitive advantage by focusing management
  attention on the key success factors;

- improving management's understanding of commercial
  operations;

- enhancing shareholder value by reducing the adverse
  impact of downside risk and maximizing upside potential;
  and

- giving senior management a clear view of the risks they are
  taking as well as those they are avoiding.

Definitions of risk

The identification and measurement of risk is covered by
many professional disciplines including engineering, actuarial, mathematics, health, environmental and financial
studies. There are numerous linkages between these
various professions and disciplines.

In the Australian Standard 4360:1995, 'Risk management' (which is being considered by the ISO as a basis for
an international standard) is defined as:

> The chance of something happening that will have an

> impact upon objectives. It is measured in terms of consequences and likelihood.
>
> Risks are uncertain future events which could influence the achievement of the organization's objectives, including strategic, operational, financial and compliance objectives.
>
> Risk defined this way can be linked to 'return', which is consistent with, for example, the views of the Institute of Chartered Accountants in England and Wales in its 1999 paper on the management of risk (the Turnbull Committee, 1999).

Risk management principles – objectives

Risk may be thought of as embodying issues that either hinder or enhance the achievement of an organization's objectives. An understanding of an organization's objectives can provide the rationale and direction for a risk management framework.

These organizational objectives are often linked to the need to satisfy those key stakeholders who may have an impact on performance or are affected by its performance. Knowledge of stakeholder needs is integral to the process of understanding an organization's objectives and value creation. A key group of stakeholders are shareholders and institutions with a particular interest in the generation of shareholder value. The relative importance of each shareholder should be assessed and understood. Figure 1.7 describes a simple matrix that can help with the prioritization process.

The generation of shareholder value is the result of complex interrelationships between growth, risk and return. Taking and managing risk is at the heart of shareholder value creation. Current approaches to shareholder value creation, however,

Figure 1.6 Risk management principles – objectives

often emphasize growth and return while paying little attention to the specific risks inherent in implementing profitable
growth strategies. Where risk is identified, many organizations
continue to rely on financially focused risk mitigation strategies such as foreign exchange and capital structure practices,
perhaps formulated when the organization's size and financial
structure were vastly different. While the stock market has
been rewarding companies for their success in creating shareholder value, new approaches are necessary to sustain current

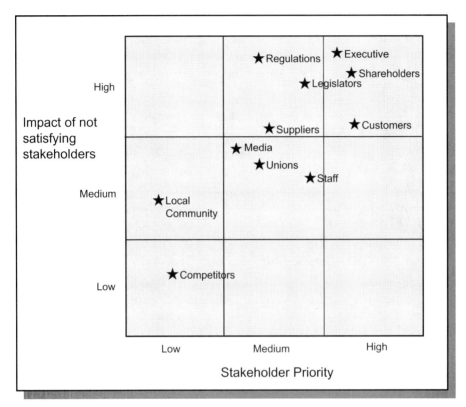

Figure 1.7 Example stakeholder analysis matrix

levels of growth. The key objective is to integrate a dynamic concept of risk into the existing focus on growth and return.

Overall, an improved awareness of the alignment of an organization's objectives and its risk profile provides a foundation from which market opportunities can be identified and shareholder value can be enhanced. Organizations should aim to evaluate their objectives at all levels – from board level mission, through to individual employee responsibilities.

Ultimately, having a clear understanding of all stakeholders' needs and especially those of the shareholders helps executives develop to a more comprehensive appreciation of the risks that may hinder the achievement of objectives.

Risk appetite

The shaping of an organization's objectives is inextricably linked to the prevailing appetite for, and tolerance of, risk. It is the role of the executive management to provide guidance on the risk appetite and tolerance that define the extent of risk taking that the organization finds acceptable.

Risk appetite may be defined as 'the risks that an organization is in business to take given the context of its corporate goals and its strategic imperatives'. Risk tolerance represents a threshold or measurement. Risk appetite may also be defined as 'the economic and operating sensitivity an organization has to risk'. When taken together, an organization's risk appetite and tolerance will determine what type of management response is necessary to manage a particular risk effectively.

In quantifying risk appetite and tolerance levels, some of the key issues to be considered include:

- What risks are the organization prepared to take in pursuit of its business objectives and what risks are unacceptable? Is the board comfortable with the level of risk taken by each of the organization's business or operating units?

- Are these risk levels consistent with the organization's strategy, business objectives, profitability targets and capital levels?

- Where should exposure to risk be reduced?

- Are some business opportunities being lost as a consequence of the management being too risk-averse? What risks should be taken to take advantage of these opportunities?

Figure 1.8 Risk management principles – risk

- How will stakeholders be affected by future and related risks that management intends to take?

While all organizations take some risks in the pursuit of their objectives, exposure to these risks must be managed. Shareholders and lenders entrust their capital to companies and their boards because they are seeking a higher return than could be achieved through risk-free low-return investment strategies (in government securities, for example). In this context, 'risk' may be defined as uncertain future events that could influence the achievement of the organization's objectives, including strategic, operational, financial and compliance objectives.

Most boards and executives are expected to demonstrate both entrepreneurship and dynamic behaviour, while assessing and managing potential risks along the way. Shareholders have an expectation that care will be taken to ensure that their investments are properly protected from day-to-day business risks, as well as those associated with the process of change. They expect management to ensure that preventative measures and contingency plans are in place – to help minimize the impact of a change failure.

Risk management principles – controls/processes

'Controls/processes' encompasses a wide range of possible management responses to risk, whether viewed as opportunity, uncertainty or hazard. They are established within a risk management framework, designed to help ensure that business objectives can be achieved (see Figure 1.9).

Controls/processes embody five interrelated components:

- control environment;
- risk assessment;
- control activities;
- information and communication; and
- monitoring.

Control environment

An effective control environment provides the discipline and structure needed for risk management to succeed. Environmental factors include:

Figure 1.9 Control/processes

- the integrity, ethical values and competence of people;

- management's philosophy and operating style;

- how management assigns authority and responsibility;

- attitude to staff training and development; and

- the direction provided by the board of directors.

Common examples of these factors include: a written code of conduct; training programmes that embody management's expectations and corporate values; incentive programmes linked to both business and risk management effectiveness; established authorization protocols; and the independence and attitude of the board of directors.

Risk assessment

Risk assessment processes need to be able to take account of change, and to account for how internal and external changes influence the objectives. Circumstances demanding close attention include:

- changed operating environment;

- new personnel;

- new or revamped information systems;

- rapid growth;

- new technology;

- new products or activities;

- corporate restructuring acquisitions divestitures; and

- foreign operations.

Control activities

Control activities should be designed to respond to risks throughout the organization, and could include a diverse range of activities specific to particular activities, such as: approvals, authorizations, verifications, operating reviews and improvements and segregation of duties. Internal audit has a key role as an independent version of control activities.

Information and communication

An essential enabler of any organization is information systems that provide a means for measuring results against objectives. These systems must be accompanied by communication practices that allow bad news to travel up to senior management, best practices to be shared across the organization, and management's intent to be understood by all. This involves the capture of information in the first place, and the bringing together of the relevant and timely data and appropriate systems.

Monitoring

Control activities and processes must be monitored, so that their quality over time can be assessed. Monitoring activities include ongoing monitoring (such as the routine supervision of clerical activities to check the division of duties between different employees) and separate evaluations (which may include internal or external audits).

These five controls/processes components are at their most effective when they form an integrated system able to react dynamically to changing conditions. The aim is to 'build in' risk management processes into the organizational infrastructure. Effective monitoring support quality and empowerment initiatives help minimize unnecessary costs and enable quick responses to changing conditions.

Risk management principles – alignment

Most organizations in today's business environment face fast and continuous change. A constant challenge for management is to align processes and strategy with the actions of employees in the face of this barrage of change. One of the key goals of 'value-based management' is to cascade these principles down through the organization. This may involve the principle of 'linkage' with senior management constantly 'walking the floor' to ascertain whether their messages are being acted upon.

Figure 1.10 Risk management principles: alignment

Alignment really refers to an appreciation that objectives drive activities; those objectives embody an organization's appetite for risk; and controls and processes respond to risk by acknowledging, communicating and managing threats and opportunities. A lack of connection within these relationships, for example, a lack of consistency between objectives and tolerance for risk, may result in organizations taking undue risk or not taking advantage of opportunities that arise.

Alignment requires, therefore, a clear overview of how the organization works and its objectives. A structure can be fitted to ensure that these objectives are fulfilled, establishing individual responsibilities and lines of accountability.

Operational risk and business change

Over the last two decades, organizations in most sectors have found it necessary to embrace a programme of almost constant change, encompassing downsizing, business process reengineering, new quality management, mergers and acquisitions activity, outsourcing, and so on. Experience has shown that an organization's exposure to operational risk tends to increase as the rate of change increases and individual change initiatives interact with each other creating an impact at the level of the organization. The rate of change can alter the risk profile of an organization and by doing so, catch management and staff by surprise.

The introduction of new technology may not be a significant source of operational risk by itself, but the secondary effects of its implementation could be. An example is the implementation of a new straight-through payments processing system involving automatic diarising and payment reconciliation. However, if this new technology is introduced at the same time as the downsizing of clerical support groups previously responsible for identifying and correcting reconciliation problems, the overall level of exposure to risk may increase. The introduction of new delivery channels – such as the Internet – may generate cost benefits, but without the necessary increase in technical staff with appropriate skills, may not be controlled effectively. The increased use of inexperienced temporary staff can also pose a risk to any business process, especially where there is limited process or control documentation.

Increasing transaction volumes, arising from increased market activity, can put pressure on businesses to perform and increase the impact of disruption. When businesses begin to operate across geographical borders and time zones, time can become a new constraint, or a window for problem solving.

The recent wave of mergers and acquisitions has increased many organizations' overall exposure to operational risk. Risk often increases during the post-deal period, when working practices, systems and corporate cultures not designed to work together are suddenly thrown together. In the longer term, there are many advantages to be gained by integrating two merged businesses in the shortest time possible, but the speed of change can mean cutting corners in a number of operational and business processes, at a time when adequate management supervision may be lacking.

The interaction between business change and broader developments can be further illustrated using a few key examples.

A large US-based computer company

In 1991, an US-based computer company suffered large losses due to a lack of good management during a period of increased revenue and expansion. The organization's entrepreneurial roots failed to expand its management team and stock control and forecasting systems were not able to keep up with demand.

While revenues soared by 43 per cent to $2.9bn in 1993, the firm still achieved losses of $36m. Analysts suggested that these losses were due to neglect of the laptop market, poor stock control, product forecasting systems not keeping up with growth, the closing of 150 suppliers and a poor distribution system.

Major distributor (France)

A major distributor developed an invoice-processing backlog over a recent Christmas period, during the busiest time of their operating year. The backlog developed following the late delivery of a major change initiative, coupled with problems arising from the implementation of a new accounting system. The backlog processing invoices ended up representing more than $100m in revenues. A further $1m lost in the system was recovered at a later date following a reconciliation exercise.

An international airline

In 1993, 16 fatal airline accidents in the Far East resulted in 346 deaths. Weather was cited as a determining factor in these accidents, with controlled flight into terrain (CFIT) the primary cause. All planes involved in the accidents were modern.

However, the airline's problem was at least partly caused by the impressive rate of air-transport expansion within its borders. This expansion applied more stress upon the air traffic control system and, in addition, on the ability of the authorities to carry out proper pilot training.

Overall, the authors have identified three interrelated causes of increased operational risk following a study of a large number of high-profile operational failures. These are:

- reduced levels of experienced management supervision;

- increasing transaction volumes, which risk swamping the operational processes; and

- changes to overall business relationships, with increasing cross-organizational dependencies and the attempt to integrate working practices, systems and cultures that were not designed to work together.

Case study: a US-based pharmaceuticals organization

This large pharmaceuticals organization has developed an innovative approach to managing the upside. From experience, it has found that its success comes largely from marketing its products. Alongside its marketing efforts, it has to make a number of claims to consumers about these products as to their health benefits. The stronger the claims, the more the products are likely to be bought. However, at the same time, strong claims carry a risk in that they may be considered excessive or inaccurate by government agencies, leading to possible lawsuits and regulatory actions.

Therefore, the organization has had to 'manage the risk' inherent in making aggressive claims about its products. It makes sure that there is evidence demonstrating that claims can be substantiated and the risks of possible actions against the organization are assessed by legal counsel. It has built up a knowledge base of the likely type of claims and circumstances that could arise. The aim of the general counsel is to 'get the lay of the land on a real-time basis'. A lawsuit or a regulatory challenge is always a possibility, and thanks to this system of risk management the board of the organization are always updated on the likelihood of such challenges.

As a result, it is possible to see that risk management creates a competitive advantage for the organization. Through better risk management, a potential hazard is transformed into a source of opportunity because the organization knows with precision the boundaries of its assertions.

Case study: a US-based biotechnology organization

This organization invests heavily in a portfolio of R&D programmes to discover new drugs. As the head of business development observed, 'I think about innovation in the context of risk.' The organization cannot avoid risk since it is central to its way of going forward and progressing.

But risk is a double-edged sword. It offers tremendous rewards – a single new successful drug may generate billions of dollars in revenues with an 85 per cent gross margin over the life of the patent. But such opportunities contain a downside. In the process of developing drugs, only about 7.5 per cent of good ideas emerge as successful commercial products. And that is after an average lead-time of around eleven years needed to develop a drug.

This risk is exacerbated because of the large capital outlay for development. On average, a biotech or pharmaceuticals organization would have spent $120–200m by the time a drug wins approval by the FDA (Food and Drug Administration) and hits the market. Because of the rigorous testing process, a drug can fall at the last hurdle, after years of development and investment.

To cope with understanding these risks adequately, the organization is developing a formal methodology assessing the probability of the success or failure of drug development projects. The business development staff compiled a comprehensive risk analysis for three points considered critical during the developmental cycle. For this, they pooled a vast amount of information relating to the technical, clinical and commercial prospects of a project. The CFO believes that over time 'these risk management techniques should shift our success rate.'

Case study: a large international pharmaceutical organization

One important risk management project at this organization, one of the world's largest pharmaceuticals companies, has been supply chain risk analysis. An industry trend of the last few years has been the outsourcing of manufacturing with a reduction in the numbers of suppliers. This has come about because companies are under increasing pressure, in the face of greater competition, to cut costs. However, this process has increased dependency on one or a few suppliers for a key raw material. This process increases risk in the supply chain which then needs to be managed.

As a result, they are assessing the supply chain from a total perspective. It is looking at the 'cradle to grave' of a product, from external supply materials through to manufacturing and distribution. By doing so it is identifying 'pinch points' – those places where there is total dependency on a manufacturing facility for the critical stages of a product's manufacture. By undergoing this type of risk assessment, it becomes possible to identify alternative suppliers, build up buffer stocks, and insure the residual risk. In effect, the goal is to ensure business continuity.

Operational risk management of this type has already given this organization competitive advantage. Regulation is especially stringent in the pharmaceuticals sector and companies can be punished for not producing health products that are always urgently required in the marketplace. A competitor of this particular organization was shut down recently by the US Food and Drug Administration for failing to supply a vaccine. The said organization stepped in and picked up the market. The fact that it did so was testament to the effectiveness of its operational risk management.

Case study: a Europe-based organization

One of Europe's largest chemical companies provides a good illustration of what operational risk management means for such an organization in the modern age. Business continuity has been recognized alongside product liability as the key risk management item. This risk is especially acute for the organization since it has one of Europe's biggest integrated chemicals sites, based in the Netherlands. Two crackers support around 50 plants which are all integrated with each other on the site. Since the European site accounts for a substantial part of the group, worldwide risk is all the more concentrated. The maximum possible loss faced by the organization – running in the billions of dollars – does not come from initial property damage caused by fire, for example, but from the loss of commercial business and the loss of reputation that the organization would suffer from. Taking out an insurance policy against fire, therefore, would not be enough protection by a long way for the organization's risk exposure.

Their approach is to take a more integrated view of risk because it has assessed where risks interact and overlap with each other. For example, the maximum possible loss from business interruption depends on where the organization is in the economic cycle, which is prone to swings in the chemicals industry. If the cycle is in a trough, demand is weak and sales are affected, whereby the exposure posed by business interruption is less. This means that it can reduce its insurance buying, for example.

> The organization's mission statement is to be 'highly competitive, safe and responsible'. To aspire to achieve these goals means examining risk from both the upside (to increase competition) and the downside (to be safe in the community).

The benefits of operational risk management

The influence of shareholders on boardrooms has grown substantially over the last two decades. Business performance is increasingly measured by reference to shareholder value. The rise in importance of financial performance benchmarks such as earnings per share growth, or economic value added (EVA), are indicative of this shift in emphasis. Boards are more inclined to invest capital in those projects where the return is greatest.

It is in this context that risk management can make a contribution towards increasing the value of a business. The main concern or risk that shareholders face is how much the accrual return on their investment differs from their expectations. Irrespective of the nature of individual risk exposure, traditional shareholders have been more preoccupied with financial volatility than with the possible hazards that could damage shareholder value. Overall, risk management practices contribute to the enhancement of shareholder value because they help to generate a business environment that is able to minimize both the likelihood and impact of risk occurrences that could decrease shareholder value and exploit opportunities to create value when they arise.

Managing for shareholder value is therefore likely to change the orientation of risk management. One, taking and managing risk is at the heart of shareholder value creation. This means that risk management cannot be too defensive and stifle risk-taking. Two, it is true that shareholders want stability;

managing risk has a vital role here but managers will need to go beyond the focus on hazards and examine how risks in total – the upside and downside – impact the balance sheet.

Many organizations continue to rely on what may be considered static financial risk mitigation strategies – such as foreign exchange and capital structuring practices, perhaps formulated for a corporate structure that itself has become superseded. New approaches are vital if organizations are to sustain their current level of success in creating shareholder value and be rewarded by the stock market.

Management must be willing to expand their approach to risk, moving beyond the existing focus on risk as hazard to embrace the opportunity and uncertainty dimensions of risk. In particular, management must be willing to explore the relationships between growth, risk and return. They need to go beyond merely taking steps to adjust return requirements for the different risks inherent in investments. Risk management needs to be considered as part of their operational assessment.

Such an approach can help to bolster the process of managing change. It can help organizations take advantage of new opportunities such as e-business, and ensure that when restructuring does take place, risk and return are optimized. These and other issues are examined in more depth in Chapter 4: Operational risk issues for the twenty-first century.

Shareholder value and operational risk management

There are a number of links between the seven drives of shareholder value and operational risk management activities:

- **Sales growth**: Organizations can alter operations to develop and introduce competitive services and products.

- **Operating profit margin**: This works at a basic level as firms reduce their operational losses. A more forward-looking

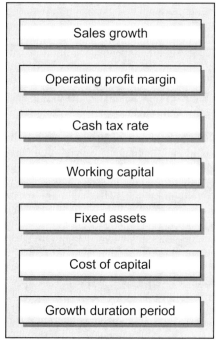

Figure 1.11 Seven drivers of shareholder value

strategy would be to develop and deliver high-value, premier products and services.

- **Cash tax rate:** Ensuring accuracy and timeliness of information.

- **Working capital:** Just-in-time stock management can lead to improved cash-flow, freeing up capital normally tied up in the business.

- **Fixed assets:** Preventative maintenance can stave off capital depreciation.

- **Cost of capital:** By preventing business interruption and making the business infrastructure more stable, firms can improve their credit risk ratings, leading to lower cost of debt.

- **Growth duration period:** By achieving greater operational efficiency through risk management, companies can grow by improving the time-to-market of their products.

More generally, the value generated by any business can be described in terms of the combination of cost, quality and timeliness (cheaper, better, faster). This definition of value also shows that any steps taken to minimize the risk of, for example, a loss of quality or late delivery of a product or service, must be balanced against the costs incurred in their execution. The timely delivery of a product, for example, may also be adversely affected if too many quality controls are required.

Cultural factors in operational risk management

Organizations will only manage risk if their members want to. That is why regulation – and self-regulation – is, to some extent, a thorny issue. Regulators can force a bank to implement a very expensive risk management system. But they cannot dictate that risk will be managed effectively. At the end of the day, the success or failure of active risk management falls on the enthusiasm and willingness of individuals to manage risk.

Often, there is a large incentive not to manage risk. This disincentive may be an integral part of an organization's culture. In banking, a counter-force some have entitled 'moral hazard' may be at play – the tendency for individuals to take excessive risks because the culture encourages it.

Similarly, a culture where nobody is willing to speak out and raise problems may mean that important risks will not be communicated to the board and to the organization's stakeholders. Board members themselves may be

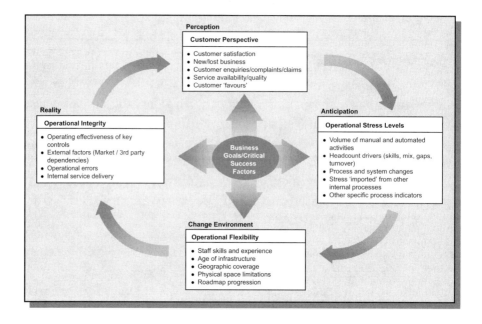

Figure 1.12 Operational resilience balanced scorecard

accused of being alarmist for wanting to make effective risk management a priority. Often, therefore, risk management is about rocking the boat and asking the unthinkable. Corporate culture frames the willingness of employees to talk openly about risk and can be the critical factor.

Operational resilience

Organizations are increasingly dependent on their operational processes being available 24 hours a day, 7 days a week. Even a brief, unplanned outage can lead to process breakdowns affecting an organization's ability to take customer orders, despatch goods or complete credit checks. For example, the non-availability of a LAN network supporting fifty staff responsible for credit approvals at a credit card organization for even a short time effectively stops the business.

As we have seen, one of the goals of operational risk management is often to ensure greater business continuity. But ORM is not merely defensive and safety-oriented. A main message of this book is that, by allowing organizations to keep a stricter rein on their operations and maintain continuity – what we have termed 'operational resilience' – ORM can enable organizations to reap significant competitive advantage.

To enable this requires not only a more detailed knowledge of business processes or operational specification. It requires

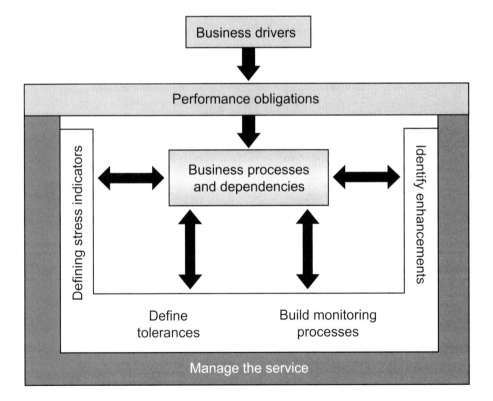

Figure 1.13 Operational resilience envelope

approaching the definition of risk in a fresh way – seeing the upside opportunity of risk as much as the downside negative impact. Further, organizations need to grasp the relationship between the two. The benefits are both immediate (greater continuity equals greater profitability and efficiency); second, firms can glean sustainable competitive advantage by building trust in the marketplace.

Operational resilience is defined as being the ability of a business process to adjust to or recover quickly from change, disturbance or misfortune. Increasingly, operational resilience is becoming critical to business survival. High-level business trends are pushing organizations to provide high-availability, round-the-clock service services or '7 × 24 operations'. These trends include:

● the expansion of e-business;

● the globalization of operations;

● the increase in remote computing use by mobile and home-based employees;

● the fierce competition in some business segments, that has driven many organizations to provide around-the-clock customer service; and

● the attempt to ensure service stability for a large number of distributed sites.

The 24-hour society

The '24-hour society', driven by technological advance, is becoming a reality. The most immediate expression is that retail outlets are open longer hours than in the past. But the 24-hour society is much more than late-night supermarkets. Work is becoming more flexible, meaning that people are increasingly working outside the traditional nine-to-five routine. Many areas in the public sector – such as schools – are experimenting with staying open longer, at weekends, in the evenings and into the night.

At the same time, electricity usage has increased in the evening and night-time and in addition, use of the telephone has also substantially increased during these later parts of the day.

On a social level, these trends are likely to accelerate as more of society makes use of the latest technology, which has the affect of enabling greater mobility and speed of communications. In short, what we are witnessing is what a recent commentator called 'a new relationship with time'.

Source: *The 24-hour Society*, Leon Kreitzman

Examples of high-resilience processes

Financial services	Telephone banking, home banking, ATM networks, payment and clearing systems
Telecommunication services	Mobile phones, pager service providers and managed data networks
Cable television companies	Pay-per-view services
Transportation service providers	Air traffic control and ticket reservation systems
Credit card companies	Card authorization systems
Warehouses	Just-in-time or automated operations
Insurance companies	Call centres
E-business	Trusted third parties

The explosive growth of e-business over the past year and the move towards globalization have together created new markets that favour those organizations that are most able to provide reliable direct channel transaction processing and fulfilment services around the clock.

Market forces have forced organizations to develop products with higher quality and increased functionality at lower cost than their competitors. These competitive forces have also pressurised organizations to reduce product-time-to-market and improve product quality, improve customer service, forge new links and strategic partnerships with suppliers, reduce inventory levels, and increase stock turnover ratios. At the same time, in many organizations, shrinking profit margins have reduced the margin for error to a minimum.

Revenue growth in many organizations is dependent upon operational processes that deliver quality products or services to customers faster than in the past. In most cases, revenue growth is accompanied by increased profitability only if the cost of delivering those products and services is managed effectively. Profits are only generated when revenues are greater than costs. This is another vital reason for the importance of operational resilience.

Rethinking operations management

In the past, many organizations have relied on 'operations management', a management discipline in its own right. Operations management focuses on the smooth and efficient running of an organization. As such, to some extent it encourages managers and staff to consider risk.

One drawback of operations management in its traditional mould, however, is that it is framed within the day-to-day operations of an organization. As a result, it often remains aloof from strategic considerations.

However, operational planning cannot be divorced from strategic planning because:

- Operations investments tend to be large and fixed, often tying up capital over a period of time where uncertainties will prevail. Once decided on, they tend to limit an organization's direction and flexibility to try other strategic routes.

- In the growing service economy, customers often interface directly with 'operations' when they buy a product or service. Receiving good service from a private health clinic is inextricably bound up with how well that clinic operates. This principle holds true across a range of service sectors, from clinics to restaurants to banks.

- Many markets are inherently unpredictable. Changing patterns of supply and demand can leave companies with excess inventory, order backlog problems, or sudden rises in demand. As a result, the core of operations needs to be protected from the instability of marketplaces. Managing capacity – the productive capability of the operations function to provide the required range of goods and services to be sold in the market – is at the heart of sound business management and is at the centre of good operational risk management. Lack of capacity during periods of high demand can lead to loss of market share, which will almost always go to a competitor. On the other hand, excess capacity means higher costs, as some part of the investment will give no return.

On another level, operational resilience can no longer be divorced from an organization's market competitiveness and reputation. This is due to more recent developments:

- Greater competition from markets is applying more and more pressure on organizations. It serves to highlight the dependency firms have on operational resilience.

- Brand value is increasingly recognized as a key way in

which businesses can differentiate themselves in the market, as other forms of competitive advantage, such as price, are no longer open to them. This means, however, that service levels to customers need to be consistently high and sufficient levels of trust established. The best competitors are not those with the cheapest labour or the best-cost structure but those that are most successful in winning and retaining new customers. To seize the opportunities of today's markets, organizations must begin to complement their cost cutting defences with revenue-generating offensives – they must recommit themselves to building business processes that improve performance in the marketplace and so generate new business.

In a growing number of businesses – financial services and telecommunications to name a few – success is driven by the ability to provide around-the-clock, high-quality services, but few companies realize just how vulnerable they are to unexpected problems. Recent outages in telecommunications services illustrate this point. One such outage disrupted hundreds of businesses, preventing cash registers from operating, knocking out ATMs, and blocking machines from verifying credit card transactions. And few companies had the backup data systems in place that would have enabled them to continue normal operations.

How can high-risk companies reduce their vulnerability and still keep costs down? The answer lies in reliable operational processes that can deliver quality services and goods to customers, without error and on time. But only a few organizations have learned the art of cutting costs while simultaneously building business processes and systems that improve performance and attract new customers. A key step towards that goal is to build processes flexible enough to cope with a rapidly evolving marketplace.

Businesses that have reduced the time-to-market for new products and services – without sacrificing quality and profitability – are gaining a critical advantage in today's competitive marketplace. To guarantee customer satisfaction, these organizations are installing and maintaining processes that have sufficient resiliency to cope with operational stress, component failures, and major disasters. While re-engineering their operations, these companies never lose focus on managing risk. For some, that means maintaining adequate staffing levels. For others, it entails outsourcing selected services in a way that retains control of those functions. And for most, it requires building infrastructures that can meet peak periods of capacity.

Focusing on risk management

After a major disaster, many organizations can be expected to make risk management a high priority. But over time, its perceived importance diminishes. Corporate vigilance wanes. Market research has shown that many organizations still do not use a co-ordinated approach to managing risk. Like the businesses inconvenienced by recent telecommunications outages, few companies have the systems ready to continue serving customers in the event of a breakdown.

Well-managed organizations manage both the downside and the upside of risk. The responsibility for ensuring that operational risk management permeates the organization rests with the senior management team. It is impossible to build a resilient organization without clearly defined management models and objectives that take advantage of effective communication channels. Senior management needs to promote the awareness and management of risk as an ongoing objective. In addition, it needs to convince stakeholders – shareholders, employees, and even customers – that risk and loss control and risk transfer are key factors in sustaining profits. Day-to-day operations also need to support risk management. To keep management informed, internal audit reports and other regular communication to senior management should include information on departmental and company-wide efforts to manage risk.

Managing the organization to achieve operational resilience is an effective means of striking a balance between cost cutting and service. Companies can manage risk for revenue growth by ensuring that defensive cost-cutting strategies do not interfere with efforts to attract, and most important, retain customers. Resilient organizations are more likely to deliver reliable, quality services and products to secure customer loyalty and generate increased revenue.

Managing risk through staffing

Risk is inseparable from business. Operational processes must be planned to absorb foreseeable regular incidents, along with the additional demands placed upon them by internally and externally driven change initiatives. In many organizations, however, the zeal for cost cutting has eroded operational buffers that provide management with the resources to handle unexpected upturns in transaction volumes or to minimize the impact of major incidents. For example, in the early 1990s, telcos forecasted a lower demand for residential phone lines, particularly in urban areas. Accordingly, they shed workers through buyout offers and layoffs. Now, many of these telcos are scrambling to meet the rising requests for second phone lines from customers seeking Internet access.

Managing risk while cutting costs

While retaining sufficient staffing levels is one way to maintain a resilient operation, many organizations are still faced with the necessity of cutting costs. Such internally driven change often introduces a wide range of operational risks. For example, several years ago, a major oil company launched an ambitious cost-cutting campaign that sought to reduce headcount in head-quarters areas such as finance and accounting. But the company operated in a multinational environment. Inaccurate or untimely financial information from its subsidiaries could have threatened its operations in those countries. The company solved this problem by outsourcing its country-based finance and accounting functions into regional shared-service centres. Working with the outsourcing provider, the company consolidated and improved its financial and accounting processes, reducing costs while continuing to deliver accurate and timely information to senior management. As a result, it was able to cut costs without increasing its exposure to risk.

Against this backdrop, operational resilience needs to be measured to ensure that performance management and capacity planning can be used to provide the operational buffers needed to cope with market volatility and change. The use of a balanced scorecard approach focusing on operational integrity and stress and flexibility measures provides management with the information needed to ensure that business and operational performance requirements are met.

Managing risk through capacity planning

Capacity planning is another feature of a resilient organization. This management tool requires organizations to install business processes that ensure that peak operational performance can be maintained during normal growth cycles and during periods of peak operating activity. This should account for planned peaks (possibly resulting from marketing campaigns), cyclical trends, as well as random events. In financial and retail services, companies depend on business processes that have to be configured to meet periods of normal and peak transaction processing. For example, credit card companies authorize significantly higher amounts of transactions during the Christmas shopping season. Any loss of revenue due to a system-wide computer crash that denied customers the use of their credit card would be disastrous. To compensate for this possibility, most major credit card companies have established backup facilities or contingency sites to ensure that transactions continue to be authorized.

Organizations need to establish clear policies that detail contingency plans for computer crashes, phone outages, or other potential failures. Returning to the example of the credit card companies, the card issuer may decide that in the event of an outage, its best course of action would be to allow merchants to approve all transactions under a set purchase limit. The resulting losses from fraud or customers who have used up their credit limit may be inconsequential compared with the potential drop-off in revenue.

Managing risk as a tool for shareholder value

Shareholder value can be damaged by bad decisions as well as by missed opportunities. Risk management enhances shareholder value because it helps to cultivate a business environment able to minimize both the likelihood and impact of system failures or unforeseen crises that would impair the organization's ability to generate revenue. Senior management should seek to ensure that its strategy for growth, protection, and realization of shareholder value is aligned with investor requirements. To that end, the internal resources allocated to risk management must continue to yield true value for the organization.

Living in a goldfish bowl – reputation and operational risk

Most global companies have an extensive network of stakeholders who may be categorized under five headings:

● shareholders who provide capital;

- employees who provide manpower;

- customers who provide revenue;

- business partners who provide co-operative agreements; and finally,

- society in general provides an overall framework for business to survive and prosper. This framework is defined and controlled by legislation, regulations and by public opinion.

Over the last few years, stakeholders have been more concerned with how organizations operate and more discerning in how they judge them. New standards of corporate, ethical and environmental behaviour have appeared as part of a general movement that has re-evaluated corporate governance practices in general. In a worst-case scenario, an organization may find itself under attack from one or more of this stakeholder groups for breaking codes of conduct. These codes of conduct invariably lie outside the normal business or market framework and focus on the wider consequences of how business interacts with the outside world. The issues that must now be considered include:

- sexual harassment;

- racial discrimination;

- age discrimination;

- discrimination against the physically and mentally handicapped;

- environmental concerns;

- use of child labour; and

- product mis-selling.

The upshot is that corporates everywhere face a risk to their reputation. This damage can be more longer lasting than a short bout of negative PR in the press. It can affect fundamentally how consumers or other stakeholders come to view the organization and its product. Sales can decline and, in the worse-case scenario, never recover. Studies have shown that unethical behaviour has a negative impact on shareholder value.

A number of factors are likely to increase the risk of damage to reputation for most organizations. The extension of the market and the growth of world trade in new and existing areas; new social interpretations of ethical behaviour; the easier access to information; and the growing importance of the media and public pressure groups in the Internet age.

Operational risk management can make a difference in this area. Companies taking leadership positions in the area of governance will enjoy positive benefits. For example, take the issue of transparency. This is fast becoming a positive attribute in the business and financial worlds. But for boards to embrace transparency, they need to have confidence in the integrity of their operational risk controls.

The two need to go hand in hand: seeing reputation as a strategic asset; and building confidence in operational integrity and delivery capabilities. The management of risk to reputation is now a growing area of focus in both developed and developing economies.

References

Kreitzman, Leon (1999) *The 24-hour Society,* Profile Books.
The Turnbull Committee (1999) Internal Control: Guidance for Directors on the Combined Code. Institute of Chartered Accountants in England and Wales.

2

Operational integrity

Introduction

To be effective, operational risk management needs to find expression in an organizational framework. Until now, managing operational risk in any systematic fashion has been very difficult. Although line managers may have been well intentioned in controlling risk in their separate functions, the absence of frameworks and all-round risk awareness from an enterprise-wide perspective has made it difficult to mitigate risk in any systematic sense.

There are two approaches to establishing effective operational risk management frameworks. The first considers the practical, basic reasons why frameworks are essential. For example, a framework should institutionalize a process where risk is managed consistently, rather than arbitrarily. It should direct people towards a common goal and understanding. And it should involve a clear division of labour and reporting lines.

These are all important objectives. There are very real dangers in not formalizing a framework. At worst, organizations remain far more vulnerable to the impact of one risk causing far more damage than it should. At best, poor integration of risk within an organization means key risk areas may be missed out. 'Integrated' risk management requires a framework where a number of different factors can be appraised at the same time. These factors include strategy, policies, organization, culture, management processes, and supporting infrastructure.

Throughout the 1990s, the increasing influence of corporate governance issues has made the issue of internal control an essential business process. A number of well-publicized corporate failures – notably the collapses of BCCI and Polly Peck in the early 1990s in the UK – spurred on efforts to find an effective system of self-regulation so that failure could be avoided in the future.

But the focus on internal controls, as many now realize, is too narrow. There is in fact a strategic opportunity inherent in establishing an operational risk management framework. That is, a framework can facilitate decision support for strategic management levels. It can be a highly effective medium through which greater information about risk can be generated for managers to use to make better decisions.

Another way of saying the same thing is that the balancing of risk and reward, rather than the creation of more internal bureaucracy, should be the prime consideration of establishing a framework.

This chapter takes this idea a step further. The overriding message is that the implementation of risk management frameworks provides a means for organizations to better achieve their business objectives. In short, frameworks can facilitate strategic decision making, rather than just focus on control for control's sake. Traditional risk management approaches do not address the need to manage risk in a forward-looking, proactive way across the organization. Internal audit, for example, traditionally focuses on financial risk rather than general business and operational factors. Internal audit is often viewed negatively, and is perceived to have a policing role rather than playing a positive role in order to improve the status of risk management within the organization. High level controls are also means to mitigate risk. But these are often applied in a reactionary way rather than facilitating a forward-looking approach.

A related positive benefit is that the adoption of frameworks from a strategic standpoint can enhance companies' external image. Publicizing high standards of risk management can confer competitive advantage. There are already signs of improved dialogue between shareholders and corporations that have adopted risk-based approaches to strategy and operations, and companies can reduce their cost of capital. Organizations that are able to demonstrate sound risk management procedures can become a more attractive prospect for investors, especially if they operate in a volatile marketplace. As a result, risk management policy could become an important factor in an organization's market value in the future. Investors may feel more comfortable for companies to embark on more risky ventures if there is greater analysis of the risks.

In many ways, this is in keeping with original objectives of corporate governance. Ultimately, corporate governance is a control system intended to provide a balance between managerial risk-taking and entrepreneurial energy with effective monitoring, so that management interests are aligned with the interests of those who have entrusted their capital to the enterprise and other stakeholders. Corporate governance also goes hand in hand with competition at the level of the global economy. The competition for resources in markets – financial, human or otherwise – dictates that they will be allocated where they will be most efficiently used. Good management complements competition.

The aim of this chapter is to provide a high-level model for establishing a risk management framework with a particular focus on operational risk. It will show that there are four key steps:

Building a supporting operational risk management architecture. This is intended to help organizations put in place the skeleton so that information can be generated in the most efficient way possible for senior decision makers to approach risk from a strategic perspective.

Establishing policy and organization. This helps to formalize the decision-making process.

Designing and implementing controls. Investments in control should be prioritized to ensure the optimum return in both the short and longer term. Management will need to ensure the expenditure on control is both aligned with strategic goals and the range of threats to the business with the end result that the business is neither over- nor under-controlled.

Creating an insurance strategy. This will assist organizations in deciding whether to retain, transfer or finance risk.

Key barriers to establishing a framework

Surveys on operational risk have shown that a number of trouble spots exist within organizations in their quest to define and manage operational risk. Some of these include:

- no consistent definition of operational risk;

- some organizations define operational risk negatively, which negates a more precise, proactive approach;

- lack of clear reporting lines. Significant operational risk issues are not escalated to the right people;

- absence of an overall policy on operational risk management;

- lack of procedures and formality. Things are done in an ad hoc way. Management of risk may be positive, but there is a lack of management as part of the overall business, and a lack of formal structure; and

- very few may have the right infrastructure to support a more formal framework.

Building a supporting operational risk management architecture

Risk management architectures are relatively easy to design, but are often not easy to implement. They depend on a number of prerequisites to succeed. This section considers factors that form the foundation for an effective operational risk management framework:

- **Senior management commitment**: The commitment of senior management to the process is fundamental to its success. Management must have an ongoing role throughout the process, commit resources and funds, and send out a consistent message to the whole organization that they are fully supportive of the risk management framework.

- **A common language and process**: Critical to the development of an integrated approach to operational risk management is a consistent language that can articulate a common process for the identification and management of risk.

A change management process owner

Building an enterprise-wide operational risk management architecture requires the development of a project implementation plan that can drive an organization through change. The project sponsor should appoint a process change owner tasked with co-ordinating the development of the project plan, reporting to senior management, facilitating the implementation, overseeing the required employee communication and training initiatives, and so on. The management of the operational risks (see Figure 2.1) associated with change should cover:

- Current business environment to monitor the impact of the change process on existing spectators and minimize the consequence of any change-related problems;

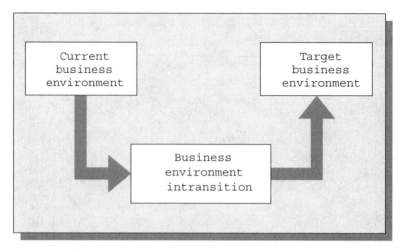

Figure 2.1 Management of changes in the business environment

- target business environment – the development of an operational risk profile of the proposed target environment can help identify process design flows at an early stage; and

- business environment in transition – the management of project-related risks affecting an organization during a change is a key aspect of operational risk management.

Establishing policy and organization

Operational risk management can only be effective when integrated into the core of operations and operating principles. The starting point for formulating this framework is to examine a range of organizational and business components as a foundation for decisive action. The key components include:

- **Strategy:** Organizations need to anticipate what they hope to achieve from putting in place an organizational risk management plan. The strategy will be conditioned by such factors as current operations, business objectives and appetite for risk taking.

- **Policy and principles:** The point of establishing a policy is to ensure a consistent approach to risk management with regard to employees' behaviour, and to ensure that all risks across an organization are identified. This is a written commitment to the establishment of a framework. The prime concern is meeting the expectations and obligations of stakeholders, whether they are shareholders, customers, regulators, business partners, competitors or non-governmental organizations (NGOs). Policies should be supported by a set of principles that apply to specific components of operational risk (such as change and project management, business continuity planning, management succession planning, and so on).

- **Organizational model:** A key element of the framework is the drawing up of a clear structure with defined operational risk management roles, responsibilities and reporting lines. The point of such a structure is to ensure that the policy (see above) is executed effectively. The structure should cover the board, committees, senior management, business and operational line management. In addition, specific operational risk management activities may be performed either by a centralized and dedicated operational risk function, or through decentralized arrangements, or a combination of the two. The nature of operational risk means that its management should be as integrated as possible into the mainstream business. It may not make sense to set up a separate group working in isolation from the rest of the organization. Management needs to anticipate how the central team will interact with the individual business units, perhaps drawing up benchmarking exercises so that smaller teams can benefit from lessons learned in different parts of the group.

- **Process portfolio:** The processes should define how action is to take place within the context of the organizational model, and should include processes such as risk identification, assessment, mitigation, reporting and measurement.

- Other factors include:
  - self-assessment and profiling;
  - executive and dedicated reporting;
  - capital allocation;
  - stress testing and key risk indicators;
  - investment appraisal; and
  - control standards.

Establishing a process for ongoing risk management

Everyone in the organization should be encouraged to take responsibility for operational risk management in his or her particular areas. The policy, design and framework for operational risk management, however, should be driven by the board and managed in the context of an enterprise risk management team. This team would be expected to have representatives at all levels of the organization, including:

- board;

- operational risk management committee;

- operational risk management team;

- business units;

- functional experts and specialists;

- line management; and

- key supervisors and staff.

Issues considered here may include those at: board; operational risk management committee; operational risk management team; and business unit levels.

The board

As representatives of the stakeholders, the board must ensure that appropriate corporate governance frameworks are established and operating. The establishment of a board-level risk management committee may be appropriate to review and endorse risk management policies and strategies, and to provide the organization with a clear focus on the management of risk.

Operational risk management committee

The key functions of a typical operational risk management committee are described below:

- To maintain the visibility of, and commitment to, effective operational risk management at the most senior management level;

- Define and maintain the policy, methodology and standards for operational risk management;

- Provide a forum for sharing organizational strategic initiatives in order to ensure that the operational risk department is able to support future change in a proactive manner;

- Provide guidance for management on conducting operational risk assessments, on improving the control of operational risks and on monitoring operational risks on an ongoing basis;

- Review periodic status reports prepared by the operational risk manager that summarize the status of initiatives and important operational risk issues. The committee members will also receive ad hoc reports and notification of significant incidents should these arise;

- Monitor developments in policy, strategy or operations that may have a significant effect on the operational risks faced by the organization;

- Monitor developments in operational risk management techniques and consider their relevance for the overall operational risk management framework;

- Assist the operational risk department to implement necessary measures across the organization;

- Act as the focal point for monitoring significant operational risks reported by the operational risk department;

- Review the effectiveness of the organization's operational risk framework;

- Monitor changes to the business and market sectors in which the organization operates, and consider the impact of these changes on the organization's operational risk framework;

- Review operational risk reports and monitor the effectiveness of management action to deal with unacceptable operational risk exposures;

- Review the impact of significant incidents, including near misses, and the appropriateness of subsequent management initiatives;

- Review and agree key performance indicators for the operational risk department;

- Approve the budget for the operational risk department and monitor actual performance against the budget; and

- Define and maintain policy and standards for organization-wide matters.

The composition of the risk committee may include directors and the risk manager. The risk manager will often act as secretary. Additional attendees may be invited at the discretion of the committee.

The frequency with which the committee meets should be determined, agreed and documented in the committee's terms of reference.

Operational risk management team

The operational risk management team is responsible for drafting operational risk management policies and strategies and typically has a performance-monitoring role. A core responsibility of the team is that risk management must be made accountable at all levels throughout the organization. The roles and responsibilities of such a team could include:

- being a primary advocate for operational risk management at the strategic and operational levels of the organization;

- providing policy, framework and methodologies to business units to assist in the identification, analysis and management of risk to ensure that business objectives are met more effectively;

- developing risk response processes to assist in the identification of the type and level of response required, and to assess the adequacy of these responses;

- facilitating, challenging and driving risk management awareness without actually being responsible for risk management at an operations unit level;

- providing assurance that the operational risk management policy and strategy set by the board is proving effective in achieving the organization's objectives;

- acting in a troubleshooting role; and

- reporting to the board or to the board's risk management committee on operational risk management issues.

Resourcing issues may include:

- cost and support required;

- skills and experience in risk management;

- career development opportunities and succession planning;

- relationship with business units; and

- information collection and management including, where appropriate, the use of specialized risk management software to record and update risk assessments.

Business units

Business unit general managers are responsible for managing risks in their particular business unit. General managers should be charged with the task of creating a risk-aware culture, where each employee is accountable for managing risk. Specific risk management obligations and performance assessments should be included to focus line management and functional specialists on risk management strategy and objectives.

Technology is one of the critical drivers of effective risk management. It can support the identification and communication of issues, or change factors, that require senior management attention. It facilitates continuous monitoring of the alignment of business units, business processes and individual activities to the organization's overall objectives. Technology also provides a process by which employees can routinely assess, communicate and manage the risks they face in performing daily activities.

Effective communication, learning and education

A communication, learning and education strategy is important to:

- introduce the concept of risk management and a business risk framework;

- educate management and employees in risk management policies and practices;

- communicate risk assessments and risk responses to the officers with responsibility for that function;

- facilitate improvement and enhancements to the risk management plan;

- facilitate and encourage regular reviews of an organization's risks;

- monitor risk management; and

- manage issues that arise.

All communications should focus on ensuring that personnel embrace the organization's risk management goals and objectives. Good communication should become an integral part of organizational culture.

Reinforcing the risk management process through human resource management

A new approach to risk management means that employees must think and behave in a different way. Making changes to organization and job design, performance reports and measures, accountabilities, reward systems and incentives can facilitate changes in behaviour.

Communications, training and leadership action can all be used to clarify new strategies, competitive contexts and values. These combine to reinforce the risk management message.

In managing the transition to risk ownership by line managers and individual employees, it is important to consider all the elements outlined above, to ensure that every part of the organization is working in support of the overall risk management strategy. If one part is not aligned, mixed messages may be sent, and anticipated benefits may be lost.

Other learning and education systems may also require refocusing. Programmes can give senior managers an opportunity to convey new risk management priorities to employees and employees' roles and responsibilities in the new risk management process and the detailed language and protocol of that process. This, in turn, helps to encourage the development of new core competencies. Information about dominant values, competitor analyses, the business environment, and the organization's future all have risk implications, which can be addressed through learning and education programmes.

Risk systems and infrastructure

An organization may need specific technical tools and systems to support the processes which provide reliable and timely information. Some examples may include expectations and failure reporting, and stress indicators.

Culture and training

A successful risk management framework, and in particular, effectiveness of the processes in that framework, is dependent on a positive enabling culture. For example, if people are prone to blame each other when things go wrong, or if whistle-blowing is not recognized as an important aspect of internal communication, then it is unlikely that information channels will function properly. The danger is that valuable information is not passed up to management, and risk exposure within an organization becomes more value threatening than it would be if managers had the information to act decisively.

Formal training sessions, workshops and internal marketing material can help to shape the right kind of culture for the success of the framework overall.

Knowledge management

It is important to ensure that systems are in place to enable employees and the organization as a whole to learn from past mistakes and missed opportunities. The rationale is that businesses can avoid making the same mistakes in the future. Ensuring that knowledge and experience are incorporated into general management planning can foster this concept of the learning organization.

Once this process is in full swing, a crucial issue is how staff access and use knowledge. For instance, knowledge may be stored in diverse databases, ad hoc reports or manuals of instruction. A knowledge management programme should ensure that this accumulated knowledge is used to greatest effect by individuals within the organization.

Communication

Complementing the cultural and knowledge components of the framework, the quality, tone and frequency of communication within an organization is a key requirement for effective operational risk management. Communication issues include how operational risk policies are communicated to staff, especially in geographically or functionally distributed organizations, and how operational risks are identified and escalated up to the appropriate level to ensure that they are addressed.

Monitoring of the risk management process

The final component of effective risk management is a reporting and monitoring structure which can ensure that risk response gaps are filled with best practices, and that the risk responses continue to operate effectively under changing conditions.

This should enable risk management activities to be monitored, aggregated and reported upwards through the organization and, ultimately, to the board. This responsibility is often given to either a dedicated risk officer, or to a sub-committee of senior managers and directors.

Internal reporting

Business risk management reporting must be carefully tuned to the various applications of business risk information. The

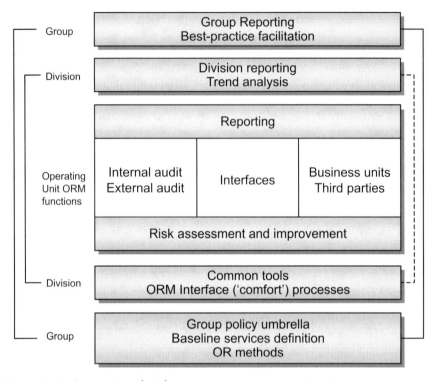

Figure 2.2 Operational risk management – organization

information must be concise, unambiguous, standardized and integrated with existing reporting processes.

Management information needs

Boardroom	Response
• Understand the extent of the organization's most significant risk exposures.	Significant organization-wide risks reported for the organization and the major business groups, including consolidated and summarized data.
• Gain comfort that the business risk management process is operating effectively.	Capacity to report emerging risks and other exceptional information and balanced status reporting (opportunities and hazards).

Boardroom	Response
• Management understand the extent of shareholder value at risk, particularly that value within the 'control' of management.	Impact measured in shareholder value terms, with an indication of which risks are controllable through management action.
• Understand how these exposures are developing over time.	Year-on-year trend analysis and comparisons.
• To be assured of the implementation of an appropriate, effective management response.	Representations by management as to the appropriateness of risk management responses can be obtained from a directors' questionnaire, possibly using a software-based assurance gathering process.

Business unit reporting	Response
• Information about significant business risks under span of responsibility.	Matrix reporting by major area of business risk.
• An indication of possible quick 'wins' in risk response implementation.	Management's relative 'control' over the risk response assessed.
• Assurance that business risk management processes are operating effectively.	Information for significant business risk drivers is analysed and held in structured databases.
• Sufficient data to monitor and assess the business risk management performance of functional reports.	Reporting by accountable manager.
• Assurance that appropriate management actions are being undertaken for the directors' questionnaire to be signed-off.	Matrices provide information for active review process of key risks and performance of functional reports.
• Renewable process to support continuous improvement.	Movement in risks over time reflected in risk profile matrices.

Individual reporting	Response
• Context and framework for understanding business risk and management business risk response.	All relevant data about risks contained in the risk database, including risk management action plan(s).
• Information about risk drivers to monitor changes in risk intensity.	Risk drivers are analysed and documented.
• Ownership of individual risks and understanding of business risk management responsibilities.	Accountabilities determined.
• Understanding the context of risk to enable continuous improvement of risk response.	Context and significance of risk established.

The role of internal audit

Organizations need to think about the role of internal audit in the context of a new and improved risk management framework. The role of internal audit, in many organizations, has moved from the compliance function to playing a major integrated role, often as the 'champion' of risk management. Internal auditors act as facilitators and mentors to management, and, as a consequence, exercise a major influence over the adoption of best practice.

External reporting

Organizations are also focusing on the need to report risk externally. The Institute of Chartered Accountants in England and Wales (ICAEW) recently proposed a process to compile a 'Statement of Business Risk'.

Operational context

A complementary approach to the framework above is to begin from a slightly different perspective. This may involve

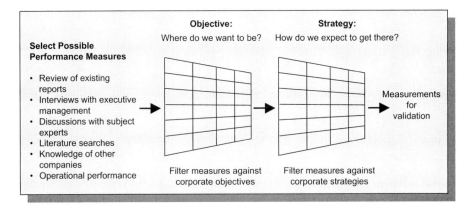

Figure 2.3 Selection of possible performance measures

examining and seeking to improve controls over existing operations. In effect, another way that risk can be managed is by implementing a control framework aligned to business goals and objectives that provides reliability, integrity and efficiency in operations as a whole.

Operations are reliant on systems, business processes, third parties, people, information, and other assets, and are subject to the intervention of management. In these areas, management can help to further the objectives of an operational risk management programme by improving project planning and scheduling, performance modelling, quality and maintenance management, capacity planning, production standards, process improvement, and cost effectiveness.

Some useful areas to examine regarding operations management practice include:

● **Workflow:** This refers to the distribution and automation of tasks in a process or series of processes. Workflow is cost-efficient and enables controls to be automated, transaction progress to be easily tracked and problems and inefficiencies to be identified. The rationalization process involved with workflow reduces human intervention and provides a mechanism for clearly defining reporting and authorization lines within the process.

- **Straight-through processing/connectivity:** This refers to the full automation of a business operation, which enables transactions to be processed from start to finish with minimal manual intervention. The advantages include cost efficient and rapid transaction processing. Connectivity with third parties (such as customers and suppliers) can lead to further efficiency gains.

- **System development and implementation:** This category includes the support and maintenance of systems. Successful implementation of systems requires adequate testing, quality assurance, change controls, and project management to ensure that systems that fully meet business requirements are available on time and within budget.

- **Transaction monitoring systems:** Financial institutions regularly process large numbers of transactions. These transactions must be monitored to ensure that they are processed completely, accurately and on time, in order to minimize penalties, and to ensure that the institution pays full attention to customer service. Monitoring systems can be designed and implemented to provide management with real time information about the precise status of each transaction, and to provide early warning of potential difficulties in processing.

- **Outsourcing/shared services:** An organization can choose to outsource part of its support activities with a view to tightening focus on core competencies, realize cost benefits, transfer risks and streamline operations. Where the organization carries out similar operational activities in a number of locations, it may also be beneficial to establish a central shared service centre to achieve economies of scale. The operational risks associated with outsourcing and shared services, however, need to be carefully managed by clearly defining measurable services, allocating responsibilities and accountabilities and establishing contracts and service.

- **Service level agreements:** The key to successful service arrangements (whether provided by third parties or delegated internally within the organization) is an unambiguous contract defining the services being provided, and the respective responsibilities of the provider and client. The agreement should define the minimum service levels, the penalties for failing to meet these, and the reporting mechanisms that will be used to assist in monitoring supplier performance.

- **Control reviews and requirements:** It is beneficial that regular reviews should analyse the control environment of an organization. The objective is to test whether business operations are conducted in a controlled manner. Such reviews should be focused on those areas of operations that are more reliant on control effectiveness.

- **Quality management:** Any product or service delivered needs to meet a defined standard. Appropriate quality assurance procedures should be in place to ensure this. Suitable quality management measures should be introduced (based on standards accepted by the industry) and be supported by adequate management reporting so that quality can be monitored on a regular basis.

- **Balanced scorecards:** Balanced scorecards allow managers to monitor business performance. From an operational perspective, they should be used at a tactical level to monitor operational performance and to verify the achievement of business goals. An operational scorecard should cover four key aspects. It should:
  - incorporate a customer perspective on operations to understand and manage client perceptions;
  - oversee operational control and integrity;
  - provide indicators of operational stress, so that management can predict and address potential operational failures; and

    – monitor the level of flexibility in operations and how well change can be managed. The major focus of the scorecard is not to measure past performance, but to either predict future problems or to provide management with diagnostics to guide their actions.

● **Risk stress indicators:** Stress indicators provide foresight of impending problems and notify management of existing problems so that corrective actions can be taken. Stress indicators should be identified and monitored to ensure they do not exceed defined thresholds that may damage business functions.

● **Data quality:** Businesses cannot perform at optimum levels, and management cannot make decisions, if data is neither accurate nor timely. In many cases, this maintenance of adequate data quality is also a regulatory requirement. Systems should be implemented to monitor errors, limits and exceptions to provide essential management reporting. Controls should be in place to ensure the reliability, integrity and availability of data.

● **Process re-engineering:** Existing business processes may be ineffective to meet the changing needs of an organization. Processes can be re-engineered to better meet business objectives, streamline operations, improve effectiveness and control, improve performance and achieve efficiency gains.

● **Cost reduction:** Operational costs can be reduced when business processes are streamlined, and potential problem areas are identified and tracked ahead of time. Cost reduction drives should be carefully planned to ensure that the right balance is struck between cost cutting and service delivery.

Case study: The Lifetrack* Project in the petrochemicals industry

Introduction

In its day-to-day operations, the petrochemicals industry has one of the highest exposures to risk of any industry sector. In this context, the transfer of operating knowledge within plants is an essential ingredient for safety and profitability. Traditional management approaches, however, focus on what may be called 'hard' technological issues and neglect 'soft' human aspects. These soft factors, such as knowledge of operations tied up in employees' heads, dialogue between staff and the learning of lessons, are essential to the risk management process. They all affect team decision making and the performance of a plant overall.

The core principle of Lifetrack is to integrate 'hard' and 'soft' factors. This means that systems support the refinement and improvement of 'soft' factors in order to improve production practice and safety. This approach is significantly different from most operations management practices. It represents a fuller integration of risk management into operational practices.

In more detail, Lifetrack provides an easily retrieved, living operational record of past incidents and lessons, drawing upon experience within the plant environment. Using electronic systems, all production staff participate in improving the reliability of operations in manufacturing plants, through striving to improve shop floor communication and the capture and sharing of operational lessons. This may be summarized as an approach that creates, and

*Lifetrack was an industrial innovation programme of the Decision Support Group in Cambridge University's Institute of Manufacturing. It started as a project supported by the UK Department of Trade and Industry (DTI), involving British Petroleum and Honeywell Control, with input from PricewaterhouseCoopers and drawing on a related DTI review of US manufacturing practice. Dr Tony Holden of the Decision Support Group and Dr Paul Wilhelmij, previously with British Petroleum and now with PricewaterhouseCoopers, initiated and led the programme.

enforces, 'corporate memory'. In essence, corporate memory refers to the ability of teams and organizations to learn from past experience and to recall key operational details for current activities and decision making.

The starting point for such a way of thinking is the observation that many organizations have inadequate memory of past events and incidents. In the process industry the most significant issue facing operating personnel today is that modern plants are so reliable that many years can pass before a shift team might experience a major event such as a planned overhaul or a compressor trip. A large number of these scenarios can be addressed by the use of high fidelity plant simulators to allow off-line training of the workforce. However, there are many situations when it is helpful to an operator, when confronted with a situation he has not previously met, to access a database to check whether the situation has been experienced by others. Providing ready access to relevant historical detail is a key feature of Lifetrack.

At the same time, there may be an absence of formal and informal networks for lesson sharing across the board. The reality of an 'inadequate memory' tends to make itself apparent whenever similar incidents or losses are repeated. A major point here is that formal review practices do not guarantee that operations employees learn from past mistakes. The truth of this statement lies in the observation that organizations continue to make the same mistakes even after mechanisms such as formal loss investigations take place.

Lifetrack consists of two elements: a systematic engagement process to identify team information needs, and an electronic system for production team members to capture operational information.

The first building block is a review process whereby questionnaires are used to build up a profile of knowledge and related organizational, information and communication factors. Figure 2.4 illus-

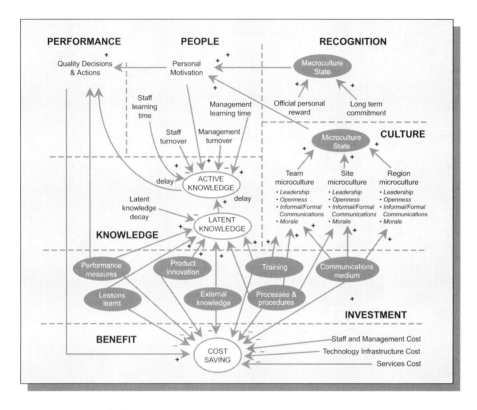

Figure 2.4 Soft factors that are potential risks to team performance

trates the factors addressed in this review. Areas of weakness identified here could be the cause of performance failure.

One of the issues addressed by the Lifetrack review is identifying key operational information required by the shift team. In practice information is often fragmented and spread across a plant. It may lie dormant in an inaccessible form or be spread about in operating manuals, plant design details, operating instructions, loss investigation reports, factory standing instructions or health and safety guidelines. As a result it may be difficult for shift teams to piece information together to get an overall picture. One of Lifetrack's overall aims is to identify key information which may

be relatively inaccessible, for example historical shift log information and incident details, and to make this information accessible
as a central working resource.

By providing focused access to key historical records, Lifetrack
helps staff manage information overload. Employees in a process
plant are presented with large amounts of data by modern plant
systems. Unless ready access is provided to supporting records,
staff will not spend time looking for key details which may help
resolve an emergency situation.

The second building block of Lifetrack is the use of an electronic
system for production team members, to record details of
occurrences or events relating to the equipment they are using.
These details could relate to identifying whether a regularly used
valve needs 'X' number of turns to close fully, when the operator
can be mislead into thinking that the valve is closed after 'X – N'
turns.

A key principle behind Lifetrack is the idea that often, lack of
human communication leads to production loss or accidents.
Experience across industry shows that miscommunication can
lead to significant financial loss. By using Lifetrack as an electronic log keeping system, different people can contribute to, and
share, the same information. This addresses a particular risk
associated with shift work. Due to the nature of the shift schedule, workers on different shifts may not be able to communicate
directly with each other. By recording details about operations
electronically, people on different shifts can be kept aware of
what has happened on a shift with which they have no direct
contact.

The Lifetrack framework

The key to Lifetrack is an all-encompassing approach bringing
together technological and human aspects. The point of integrating hard and soft aspects is that the information infrastructure is

supportive, rather than constraining, in managing operational risk. The main contribution is a vehicle to address operational risk by integrating the key pillars of knowledge management – organizational information, communication and memory – with workfloor social processes.

The following are features of the Lifetrack approach:

- a review framework to assess team knowledge factors and information requirements;

- by addressing soft factors in the operational environment of a team, the risk of operational failure relating to miscommunication and poor knowledge of past records is reduced;

- by providing a more formal means of recording what was covered at shift handover, a framework to improve knowledge sharing and shift communication within the operational environment; and

- an illustration of how computer-based tools and electronic access to plant information can improve operational practice for operators and for others.

The potential operational benefits of applying the Lifetrack approach include:

- better plant reliability, reduced disturbance impact and improved plant performance;

- improved operator awareness and confidence, with an operational team more aware of historical records and better able to learn operational lessons;

- more effective communication across shifts, including shift handover and between teams and groups within and outside the plant;

- should this information be included in the electronic system, better access to comprehensible loss investigation reports, information on lessons learnt and related documents for operational staff; and

● equipment damage limitation and maintenance savings.

Lifetrack's approach to knowledge management

Knowledge management is a key theme of Lifetrack. Each industry has a wealth of history. Similarly, each plant has its own reservoir of knowledge that can be used as a guide to present and future decision making. From an operational risk management perspective, the key is to unearth this knowledge and find ways to use it to generate value.

Many companies are now finding that the rationalization process, of cutting costs and investment in their core business, and 'downsizing' staff, exposes them to the risk of losing valuable know-how which is a resource that contributes to the growth and success of the organization. They are beginning to recognize that it is expertise, know-how, information, and data that employees use to make decisions.

At the same time, many organizations have moved to (or wish to move to) a flatter, less hierarchical structure where employees are organized into teams. Such a structure tends to put a premium on knowledge sharing and communication. Indeed, in the recent bout of restructuring undertaken by companies, there has been an attempt to use knowledge more effectively by introducing team working and giving people more responsibilities. Overall, then, 'knowledge management', as it has come to be known, is now seen as a key driver of business performance.

There is a very real reason why this issue may be neglected, however. Knowledge is a difficult resource to identify and manage. It is often difficult to analyse, and quantify, the benefit of investing in what may be called 'the knowledge resource'. The usual approach is to focus on the 'hard' issues of IT. As identified above, however, this approach can often be too narrow. 'Soft' factors such as staff turnover and motivation, openness, informal and formal communications and the working environment are critical in knowledge management practices.

However intangible knowledge seems to be, the issue of knowledge and its transfer is a very real one. In process operations, cross-shift communication is a practical example of a critical knowledge sharing process. Lifetrack supports this activity using a shift hand-over log to capture information, which can be fed into a special reporting system. This is a way to aid knowledge transfer with a view to preventing errors. However it does not eliminate the need for one-to-one discussion at handover, it simply provides a more formal means of recording what was said.

It is easy to see how failure to pass on knowledge could be magnified further if, for example, restructuring from a merger leads to the existence of different working cultures within a plant environment. These working cultures may have different styles of handing over shifts, differ in the amount of problems people are prepared to report, and so on.

It is the responsibility of management to provide ready access to this knowledge for the benefit of operational teams. These teams, which understand the operating environment better than management, can then 'make this knowledge mean something' in the day-to-day management of risk. Another issue is that the knowledge of a particular plant is spread over very different teams in various locations. Contractors, technology providers, and consultants and suppliers have this knowledge and may be located in different parts of the world. Common operational approaches and practices across the industry are therefore needed to apply this knowledge to practical operational situations. The reuse of knowledge and ongoing application of lessons from past experiences is of particular importance to safe operational practice.

Knowledge transfer at the international level is a key issue because of the increase in international joint ventures. In the spirit of Lifetrack, such transfer is not merely a case of installing state of the art technology or machinery and processes in another country. It also requires the associated transfer of associated skills and operational know-how. However the difficulty here is deciding what knowledge needs to be transferred. An electronic tool alone does not provide a solution because the value of human contact in knowledge transfer cannot be replicated by a machine.

Making the link between effective knowledge management and risk management involves:

- Developing a training programme to encourage open communication, knowledge sharing, and problem solving among teams working in operations;

- Developing the right environment for people to work together in teams in plants. This improves decision-making and can contribute to a greater safety culture;

- Paying as much attention to the organizational environment in order to achieve quality decisions, as opposed to investing in more sophisticated IT systems, which may not be the answer. Investing in IT for its own sake can be a knee-jerk reaction. Companies must consider the intangibles. Often, the work is to make the intangibles tangible; and

- Ensuring that different operational teams – production shifts, engineering staff, and management – do not work at cross-purposes. Effective sharing of operational knowledge on shift activities, lessons and highlights is therefore important. A key issue is embedding communication and information processes in operational practice to create, transfer and store knowledge.

Instituting Lifetrack

Lifetrack's electronic system and operational work framework was piloted at one of BP's petrochemical plants at Grangemouth in Scotland, providing a foundation for integrating knowledge management and supporting electronic practices into production activities. The electronic log is now a proven operational system used in four Grangemouth plants.

At Grangemouth the Lifetrack tool is generally used by Team Leaders as a means of electronic logging. Its search facilities enable historical information on a particular aspect to be retrieved, but the potential for use as a tool to allow incidents to be networked in a broader operational context has still to be developed. As with any electronic tool used for decision making, the quality of the information presented to the user relies completely on the information entered into the system. The Lifetrack system currently in use could be improved by providing better guidelines on the specific operational information to enter and the formats that should be used.

The Lifetrack review process has also been applied within new joint venture petrochemical operations in South East Asia, where lessons were applied from Grangemouth in order to improve communication and knowledge sharing at management and shop floor levels.

Drawing on lessons from these operational applications, the following measures are key to instituting the Lifetrack framework:

- putting in place decision support techniques and technology that facilitate peer-to-peer sharing of lessons and the enhancement of corporate memory at the level of the operator team, including cross-shift communication;

- encouraging peer-to-peer operational links to improve awareness of practices within plants and between plants – maintaining the value of human contact and using electronic tools to support, not replace, people; and

- encouraging co-operative development of processes, and information formats, which are compatible across the industry. Government and regulatory bodies have a role in encouraging cross-industry processes and networks, and the adoption of a framework to help transfer operational knowledge effectively.

Applying Lifetrack within a process operation to address knowledge and other intangible factors reduces operational risk and provides tangible performance benefits. Such a framework encapsulates key requirements for improved production practice and risk management in the process industry.

Designing and implementing operational controls

Exposure to operational risks can be reduced to acceptable levels by the implementation of risk improvement measures and controls. Risk improvement measures are strategic or operational controls applied to the business processes, based upon the importance of the process and associated data to the business and the value of the actual impact loss. Most importantly, controls should be aligned with an organization's business objectives.

An additional constraint is likely to exist in reality, which is the budget available to implement controls. The implementation of risk improvement measures consists of the following activities, drawing on previous business and risk analysis phases where appropriate:

- **Business process criticality assessment:** The key business processes or functions are identified for which controls must be implemented to improve risk exposure, based upon the value attributed to the loss or disruption of each process. Non-critical processes will therefore attract a lower priority for controls.

- **Threat analysis:** The likelihood and business impact of threats are analysed to determine the value attributed to the loss arising from each occurrence.

- **Net risk analysis:** The net operational risk includes the mitigating effects of existing controls that are in place, based upon the control effectiveness in reducing threat likelihood and impact loss. At this point, a risk model can be derived to indicate the net risk associated with every business threat and the gaps and omissions in control effectiveness.

- **Risk improvement selection:** The operational risk model is used to identify where the organization is exposed to unacceptable levels of risk. New control options must be subjected to:

  - effectiveness assessment;

  - implementation cost assessment;

  - cost/benefit evaluation and prioritization based on risk severity;

  - selection and approval based on budget constraints;

  - implementation; and

  - maintenance and testing.

Proposed risk improvements may typically have the following attributes:

- be cost justified, via cost/benefit or risk capital allocation methods, based upon the value of the impact loss being greater than the full cost of control implementation;

- be the most cost-effective control option;

- if control effectiveness varies with time or varying circumstances, it must ensure acceptable levels of effectiveness are reached; and

- the control is subject to periodic testing or review.

Creating an insurance strategy

Organizations have three main options when choosing an insurance strategy. These are:

- **Risk retention:** This can either mean proactive management of risk through loss control, or establishing an internal provision for loss, or both.

- **Risk transfer:** Insurance is the most popular form of risk transfer involving the outsourcing of the funding of a loss to a third party.

- **Risk financing:** Risk financing can involve a mixture of both approaches above. For example, re-insurance for low-frequency, high-severity risks such as natural disasters involves a retention of risk on the initial loss layers and a transfer of risk on the higher layers.

The first and most basic decision facing an organization is whether to hedge or not. The classic case for not hedging was made a number of years ago in financial economics. Shareholders, through diversifying their investment portfolios, can hedge risk themselves. In this scenario, it is better that firms concentrate on their core competencies: there is a danger that hedging will destroy value if shareholders diversify investments themselves.

Clearly, some risks are outside the control of management but have an important, on-going impact on business operations. Hedging these risks, therefore, is central to the project of responsible management in general. A classic example is the energy sector. As organizations within energy are partly dependent on commodity prices for success or failure, it is not surprising that hedging practices are among the most advanced in industry. Not hedging poses a risk of volatility for shareholders – who should be aware that hedging strategies might be needed to create operational stability. Businesses in cyclical sectors may face a similar problem.

The next stage involves making a distinction between high-frequency, low-severity, and low-frequency, high-severity risks. Organizations with high turnovers seek to retain high-fre-

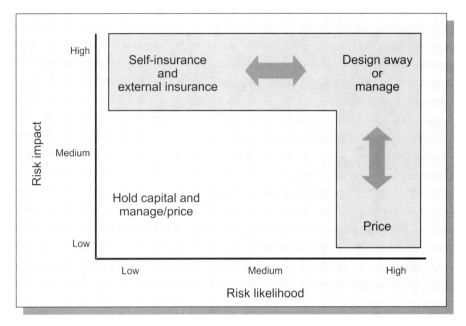

Figure 2.5 Insurance strategy model

quency, low-severity risks that pose a regular, but low-level, financial loss to the organization. Most organizations can quantify the magnitude of this loss and then put in place methods to proactively 'manage down' the risk and the loss.

In fact, as organizations have become more proactive in managing risk, they have decided to retain more risk rather than transfer risk to third parties, traditionally large insurers. As multinational corporations have developed in size and have increasing resources at their disposal, they have realized that 'self-insurance' – the setting up of an internal fund, or provision, for loss can be a far more efficient way of financing risk. This also has the advantage of avoiding the increasingly pointless routine 'trading dollars', where an insured pays an insurer premium for high-frequency, low-severity risks one year and is paid back the same amount through the claims processing procedure the next. By self-insuring, some organizations have reported savings of millions of dollars in insurance premiums.

In addition, many large organizations have their own, customized insurance companies in the shape of offshore captives that can better address their particular needs.

There are at least three other deficiencies with insurance. The first is that insurance has come to be associated with irresponsible behaviour. In the past, buying insurance was often an excuse for not managing risk proactively. Today, however, such an approach is clearly becoming untenable.

Second, insurance is not necessarily the best financial instrument to maximize shareholder value. For a start, insurance poses a credit risk, in that there is no guarantee that claims will be paid. At best, policyholders could be subject to lengthy delays before payment is made. Shareholders, on the other hand, increasingly expect minimal cash flow volatility. In the event of a disaster and financial distress, compensation through insurance could add to the uncertainty about an organization's ability to recover. Additionally, research has shown that the presence of insurance cover is not a factor in the ability of corporations to recover their share price after a disaster.

Third, many organizations now seek cover for 'intangible' assets such as brand protection, reputation, and intellectual property. Risk managers now believe, for instance, that damage to reputation is a far greater risk and more crippling to organizational success in the long term than a factory burning down, which can be replaced in a matter of months. Traditionally, however, the insurance industry has focused on hazards or perils. Many organizations have now become disillusioned with lack of innovation (and customization) within insurance markets and have turned to alternative solutions (in the form of alternative risk transfer – see later).

Insurance, then, is often viewed as too defensive for today's economic climate of harsh competition, and increasing pressures on management to deliver performance improvement and shareholder value.

At first glance, operational risk may appear to be the least amenable to some form of insurance, as many risks can be proactively 'risk managed' physically through people, resources and management techniques. However, organizational change is leaving organizations open to new risk exposures. Reengineering, mergers and acquisitions, new investment projects and divestitures, and changes in ownership structure all expose organizations to operational risks that may only have an impact later on. A classic example would be the inheritance of liabilities when one organization acquires another.

An integrated approach to financing risk

A new trend in the area of risk financing is the integrated approach to both financial and insurance risks. Traditionally, organizations have tended to approach risk from a separate, departmental perspective. The risk manager has tended to buy insurance, while the treasurer has traditionally hedged financial variables that may have an impact on the organization, such as interest rate volatility, and currency rate volatility. However, managers now have a better awareness of how risks in their 'risk portfolio' impact on one another. In this scenario, it may be inefficient to buy insurance when a gain in another part of an organization offsets that loss. Consider a (slightly extreme) real life example. A French luxury goods firm believed it would make a large loss after the Kobe earthquake in Japan destroyed property. However, this loss amounted to nothing because its brandy sales spiralled upwards as a binge of drinking followed the earthquake. Risk analysis can reveal the many examples of how risks interact. If an organization suffers a loss, but interest rates move in its favour, the two events may balance each other out.

This integrated approach is becoming increasingly important, as organizations want to show they are managing risk in a con-

sistent fashion to shareholders. For example, if speculation in
the treasury department involves a high degree of risk taking,
it may be at odds with the over-purchase of insurance, which
signals risk aversion. Shareholders, who recognize that a consistent approach across an organization signals good management, may believe that such an approach does not maximize
value.

Risk financing and shareholder value

Continuing this theme, it has already been proved that new,
innovative risk financing techniques for operational risks can
immediately increase shareholder value. An example is financing environmental remediation costs. Many firms across
sectors are affected by environmental liabilities. Some innovative products 'ring fence' or cap these costs and in the process,
remove uncertainty for shareholders by removing the need to
hold an on-balance-sheet loss provision.

One example of a recent, publicly known deal involves the
financing of off-balance-sheet liabilities for a building materials organization. This was a deal that provided $800m cover
for environmental remediation costs in excess of $100m of
costs retained by the organization. Here, a finite risk contract
was employed (implying a limit on how much the insurer
should pay) in the context of a risk financing, rather than risk
transfer, arrangement. This meant that both parties shared
responsibility for risk but also shared the upside. There was a
profit sharing scheme with respect to the investment gains
made on the new provision set aside off-balance-sheet. In a
similar deal arranged for an organization that financed the risk
of liability claims arising from asbestos damage, the share
price climbed 23 per cent in the few minutes after the deal's
announcement, and up to 40 per cent at the end of the week's
trading.

Financing operational risk in the banking sector

Innovative re/insurance service providers are now turning their attention to financing operational risk for banks, following the rise in interest in operational risk management. This is a challenging area. Banks voluntarily take on risk and retain risk. In this context, transferring risk runs counter to their core business and objectives. However, banks are now exploring alternative risk transfer strategies, in conjunction with the re-insurance market. They are exploring the use of debt and equity, alongside conventional insurance, to finance potential losses. Such losses may be associated with:

- people-related risks, such as motivation;

- property risks;

- fraud;

- financial markets catastrophe; and

- technology risk.

Equity, for example, can be used for risk financing. It provides liquidity, and if used for funding loss, could potentially be more capital efficient when compared to the alternatives of debt and insurance. Excess equity, however, does not create extra value and is costly. Insurance provides liquidity, but insurance markets impose restrictions on the types of risk that can be insured. In addition, pricing may be inefficient. Which choice of risk financing is appropriate may depend on an organization's particular capital structure.

Alternative risk transfer strategies

A wide range of innovative, 'alternative' products are available to organizations to hedge and finance risk. The main ones include:

Multi-year, multi-line insurance products

These products integrate different insurance risks, such as property and liability, into a single programme. The more advanced integrate financial and insurance risks, such as commodity hedges embedded in insurance programmes. Multi-year, multi-line products dispense with the conventional approach to insurance by packaging up different risks over a longer period of time. The result is a greater partnership approach between insurer and insured. Organizations that assume or retain more risk often find that they can get the interest of the insurance market in risks that are not conventionally insurable. For example, this approach has been popular for organizations in fast-moving sectors such as software, where there is a demand for protection against risks such as late arrival of products when they have been promised (and the consequence of paying fines for missed deadlines) and patent infringement.

Finite risk programmes

These products involve a financing deal between insured and insurer and avoid the 'win-lose' proposition of conventional 'risk transfer' arrangements. For instance, a fund set aside for loss is invested, with both parties enjoying the investment gains if no claim is made. A principle at work similar to multi-year, multi-line programmes is that once the insured accepts greater risk retention, the market is more amenable to insuring 'hard-to-insure' risks

Derivatives

A variety of new derivatives are now available which give organizations more choice. One example is the emerging 'weather derivatives' market. Simply put, many organizations in a range of sectors are affected by changing weather conditions. Energy companies are dependent on the weather for their capacity planning. If a warm winter occurs, for example, gas companies will lose sales. Weather derivatives, which are linked to independent temperature indexes, can help managers to hedge this risk. Other organizations are exploring the application of these instruments. Retail outlets, for example, are often dependent on seasonal variations for their sales, especially in the clothing business. Leisure firms depend on the weather for the success of their resorts, as another example.

3

Operational delivery

Introduction

In the last twenty years, businesses have sought to increase the speed of service delivery to the customer in a bid to gain competitive advantage. For instance, manufacturers have realized that, in an age where products become obsolete more quickly, reducing time-to-market and inventory stock levels, instituting integrated just-in-time production and delivery processes, can make the difference between success and failure. As discussed in Chapter 1, customers have become more uncompromising, wanting and demanding increasing levels of quality service.

Risk management has, traditionally, not oriented itself to this objective. But trends suggest that as managers deal with increasing uncertainty in their marketplace, they will begin to forge links between risk management and improved customer service.

In Chapter 1, we characterized 'service delivery' as 'the organization's ability to perform business processes on an ongoing basis'. The success or failure to maintain operational continuity is dependent on the effectiveness of a wide range of operational and management practices. In this chapter, we examine:

1 Capacity management.

2 Human resource management.

3 Supplier management.

4 Service management.

5 Sourcing management.

6 Project management.

7 Crisis management.

These areas cover the gamut of risks that organizations face in their bid to improve the speed and quality of service delivery to customers, from the 'high-frequency, low-severity' risks inherent in small-scale operational incidents, to the 'low-frequency, high-severity' risks that can cause a crisis and bring them down.

The starting point for managing risk in these areas is an understanding that operational issues have a direct bearing on strategic management. Continuity of operations determines the context in which managers can manage. More particularly, failure at the operational level has a knock-on effect at the strategic level. Running smooth operations gives managers more time and choice to make better decisions. Ongoing operational risk management can generate the right information so that managers can fine-tune their tolerance, or appetite, for risk-taking in the future.

The key aim is being able to better control the quality and continuity of service to the customer. Today's organizations are finding that customer satisfaction is becoming the key 'differentiator' separating them from the competition. Operational risk management can play a vital role in ensuring that managers can systematically improve customer service by ensuring that they have a strict rein over operations and service delivery.

We have mediated this message through the various sections in this chapter:

● **Capacity management:** Managing demand and supply is critical to the timely delivery of a product or service to the customer, and ensures that the risks associated with operational business processes are managed to an acceptable level and bottlenecks are avoided.

- **Human resource management:** Operational continuity and delivery of service is as much dependent on the 'continuity' of human assets as it is of physical assets. In other words, if a culture exists where people are not motivated, the ability of the organization to deliver the service effectively will be called into question.

- **Supplier management:** Control and management of risk in the supply chain is an essential part of ensuring that the product is delivered in the most efficient way possible to the customer.

- **Service management:** Organizations want to ensure that their IT systems are an asset and do not become a liability, in the understanding that IT is now far more critical to the success and operational continuity of business operations.

- **Sourcing management:** Outsourcing is becoming an important way in which businesses can achieve their strategic objectives, but they can only do this if they do not suffer a loss of control over increasingly key processes, assets and people. Operational risk management has a key role to play in ensuring that this does not happen.

- **Project management:** The creation of a project supporting culture and the management of project related risks. Projects are absolutely vital if organizations are to achieve change and progress in their marketplace. Projects are a classic case of where strategic aims depend heavily on the continuity of operations and ability of people to meet deadlines. Linking strategy and operational oversight is a key objective, then, of operational risk management in this area.

- **Crisis management:** When crises occur, one of the main dangers that organizations face is a loss of reputation, with plummeting sales of their product or service in the market.

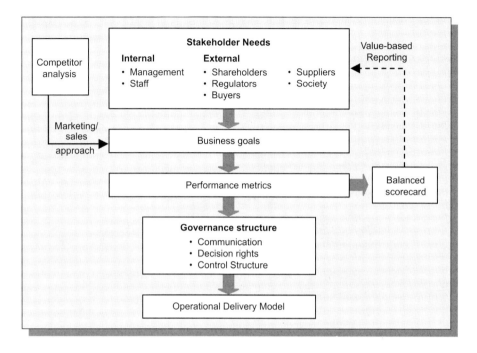

Figure 3.1 Linking shareholder needs to an operational delivery model

Crisis management can play a key role in both ensuring operational recovery and safeguarding the reputation of products in the marketplace.

Capacity management

Introduction

The 'capacity' of an organization is its ability to mobilize its resources to generate output (supply) and satisfy market demand. Capacity planning involves estimating future capacity in the context of a dynamic market environment. Levels of demand may fluctuate, either leaving organizations with too much capacity because of low demand, or stretching their resources to unreasonable limits. If resources are allocated badly, or business processes do not work in tandem with each other, operational inefficiency will be exposed in times of above-average demand. After an estimation of future needs, capacity can be either increased, say, through a new investment in plant, or cut back if supply is outpacing demand.

An effective capacity planning process should be designed so that:

- the correct level of internal and external resources are available to meet and support business needs;

- risks associated with operating business processes are managed at an acceptable level;

- resources are optimized so that business objectives are met with minimal cost;

- an appropriate level of consistency, reliability and predictability is designed into operations; and

- changes can be implemented without adversely affecting ongoing operations.

Operational resilience

There is a direct relationship between capacity management and what we term 'operational resilience' (see Chapter 1). In today's economic climate, all organizations need to operate as near to their full capacity as possible, in order to increase productivity over and above competitor levels and in the process, increase sales and profitability. However, over-stretching operations increases the risk of business interruption. Staff may become stressed, demoralized, and more prone to make errors. Equipment not built for increased output will be more prone to fault.

This tension – between maximizing profitability, ensuring high continuity levels but avoiding unnecessary operational stress –

has increased, due to factors identified in Chapter 1. This puts a premium on avoiding business interruption. By ensuring that bottlenecks in the system do not occur, and that organizations can meet their delivery and service agreements, capacity planning is key.

Overall then, organizations requiring high levels of operational resilience should develop appropriate capacity planning processes to ensure that the business can meet demands placed on it by growth, peak demand periods and unexpected changes in demand.

Organizations become immediately aware when capacity needs are misjudged. The obvious signs are:

- **Bottlenecks:** The chances of a bottleneck happening depend on how business processes relate within an organization. A hospital may have 1000 spare beds, for example. But the available capacity may only be 800, because the admissions section may only be able to process a certain number that produces peak occupancy of 800.

- **Overcapacity:** This can lead to as much inefficiency as a bottleneck. A hospital with fifty beds in a small town where the average bed occupancy is eight, with a peak of sixteen, will result in over capacity and a waste of resources, for example.

If severe, bottlenecks cause discontinuity, lost sales, and impair quality of customer service. Worse, they may damage reputation in the marketplace. At the retail level, bottlenecks immediately expose poor operational management and control. Consumers are sensitive to this. For example, the most apparent bottlenecks surface in the form of queues, at a cinema, on the motorway or in waiting for a table in a restaurant.

To ensure operational resilience, sufficient capacity must be designed and built in to operational processes to enable sus-

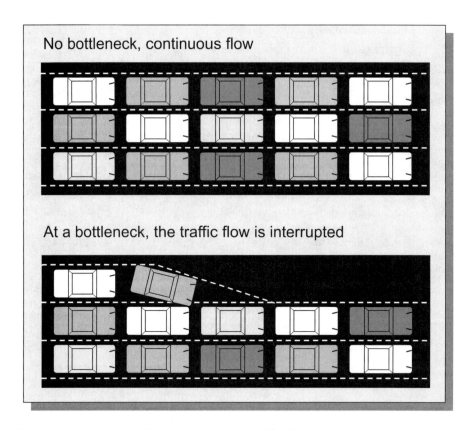

Figure 3.2 Impact of bottlenecks on traffic flows

tained growth, meet peak demand and, as a result, achieve continued profitability.

The level of resources expended implementing effective capacity planning process within an organization need to be closely linked to business goals and the need for operational resilience. A focused approach to capacity planning should enable an organization to:

● maintain or improve customer service levels;

● reduce or prevent business process or service outages;

● reduce the overall costs of overhead resources;

- improve flexibility to meet current and future needs; increase customer satisfaction levels; and

- be proactive in managing resources to meet changing demand.

Some strategic aspects of capacity planning are short-term, for example, to cover periods of expected higher demand. Retail outlets often hire extra staff or encourage overtime working over the Christmas period.

Case study: a lottery company

The volume of sales of lottery tickets tends to reach a peak in the period just before ticket sales are stopped. In general, however, capacity planning is a strategic rather than tactical function. Judging how much capacity is needed on the basis of estimates of future market demand and current operational ability is at the core of business management and is strongly linked to strategic investment decisions.

This places a considerable burden on the designers of the system and networks supporting national lotteries on the volume of sales increases dramatically as the cut-off time for sales approaches. In the event of a roll over, the volume of sales tends to increase even further.

Such decisions may be informed by managers' expectations of an organization's growth prospects in a particular industry. Managerial risk appetite plays a key role; confidence in both organizational ability and future demand in the marketplace will tend to imply generous provisions for adding extra capacity in the present and future. Growth may be organic in nature

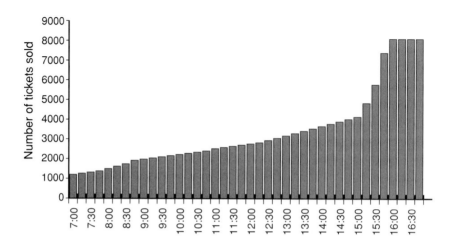

Figure 3.3 Lottery ticket sales

and subject to variations because of economic and market influences; growth may also occur as a result of the introduction of new products, or an expansion into new markets. Peak capacity demands may be cyclical due to seasonal activity, random due to external influences outside an organization's control or predictable as the result of one-off events. At times of recession, low growth and low demand, however, organizations can find that they suddenly have too much capacity, leading to declining costs and profitability.

Capacity management issues impact service, utilities and manufacturing organizations in similar ways. However, the options available to respond to these changes will vary according to each specific type of industry. Each business process works as a micro-organization, each needing to manage capacity within its own micro-environment, while under the influences of the same macro-environment.

Capacity planning

In principle, capacity planning should be straightforward, requiring a forecast of long-term demand and the provision of enough capacity to meet this demand. In reality, the uncertainties – and the risks – are numerous.

On the supply side, it may be hard to gauge the amount of product made by a particular process, because of variables such as how hard people work, number of interruptions, quality standards required, efficiency of equipment, and management ability and pressure. Business processes rarely work under ideal conditions. As a result, it is rare that operations will ever work to their full capacity. This constraint is exacerbated by the fact that in many markets, demand often comes in irregular periods, making the matching up with supply difficult. This uncertainty is central to the market economy and central to how businesses operate.

Integrating capacity and demand management

In practice, there is a need to manage both demand and capacity. Demand is often managed by focused sales and marketing initiatives. The integration of sales and marketing strategy development with capacity management techniques is vital.

Taking a simple example, a ski lift may have a capacity of 600 people an hour. But it is unlikely that all the seats can ever be filled and used because most people arrive in groups. In addition, new skiers who cannot get onto the lift first time will bring the system to a grinding halt. The effective capacity of the lift may go down to 400 people. When analysed, it is usual that one element of an operation causes a bottleneck. This element then ends up limiting the capacity of the overall operation. If a restaurant can cook 200 meals a night but only seat 100 people, it is the seating that causes the bottleneck. In this context, improving efficiency in the kitchen would be a waste of effort.

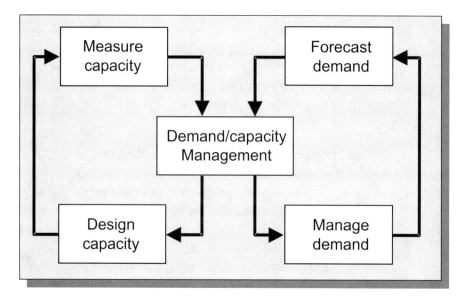

Figure 3.4 Capacity planning management model

The key is to identify where constraints lie in operational processes. Through identifying these constraints in the ongoing synergy of business processes, organizations can achieve greater efficiency and take more risks.

As the above example shows, however, wrong business processes are often identified as the key constraint on the overall operation. Some simple examples include:

● Companies increase the size of customer waiting areas, when they should be serving customers faster;

● Manufacturers recruit more sales people, when current production is too low, giving long lead times; and

● Organizations may recruit more managers when they are short of workers to do jobs.

Adding extra capacity

The following factors need to be assessed:

- **Demand** – forecast sales; sales already made; back orders; variation in demand;

- **Operations** – machine capacity and utilization; aim of stable production; plans for new equipment; use of subcontractors; productivity targets;

- **Materials** – availability of raw materials; inventory policies; current inventory levels; constraints on storage;

- **Finance** – costs; cash-flows; financing arrangements; exchange rates and general economic environment;

- **HR** – workforce levels; skill and productivity levels; unemployment rates; hiring and training policies; and

- **Marketing** – reliability of forecasts; competition; plans for new production; product substitution.

Strategies for matching supply and demand

- Capacity can more or less match demand, so that sometimes there is spare capacity and sometimes a shortage.

- Capacity can be made at least equal to demand at all times, requiring more investment in facilities.

- Capacity can be delayed and only added when it would be fully used, which needs lower investment and gives high utilization, but restricts output.

Some factors encourage organizations to increase capacity early on:

- uneven demand;
- high profits;
- the early success of a new product;
- a continuously changing product mix;
- low cost of spare capacity; and
- a need for dependable but flexible operations.

The cost of adding capacity is an important consideration. A retail outlet can hire new staff without worrying too much about cost issues. If it does run into over-capacity, and it is overstaffed, the ramifications may not be too significant.

Complex and large manufacturing companies often delay making major investments because of high cost and the knowledge that making the wrong decision may make more of a difference to an organization's performance and prospects.

Industry requirements

Financial and retail service providers are highly dependent on business systems to carry out normal business activities. The ability of these business systems to meet changing capacity requirements may depend upon the capacity and design of the underlying computer systems and data networks that support them. The business processes that support industries in the service sector need to be configured to meet periods of both normal and peak transaction processing.

Capacity management in financial and retail services and utilities

Utility service providers such as telecommunication companies, electricity generators, gas and water suppliers depend on the capacity of their distribution infrastructure to deliver services to industrial and commercial customers. These organizations need to ensure that sufficient resilience and capacity is built into the distribution infrastructure to meet current and future demand.

Building spare capacity will involve strategic decision making, consideration of likely future demand, changing technologies and the economies of scale achieved by implementing spare capacity in a single installation (e.g. laying fibre cable capacity or new pipelines). This type of capital expenditure infrastructure project often involves large expenditure and may take years to implement. The ability to predict successfully and manage future capacity requirements is critical for organizations in this sector. The absence of effective capacity planning processes can result in lost revenue, poor customer service levels or delivery failure and affecting bottom-line profitability.

Designing capacity planning processes

In designing capacity planning processes managers need to consider all aspects of operations which affect operational performance, such as:

- Balancing the *cost* of providing additional capacity against demand. Where capacity consistently exceeds demand, this could result in higher costs per unit and under-utilization of resources.

- Ensuring that sufficient capacity exists to satisfy demand at any point in time to ensure that *revenues* and *speed and reliability of service* are maximized.

- Avoiding adverse effects on *working capital* caused as a result of building up of finished goods inventory or through investment in resources (e.g. staff, IT systems, machinery) in advance of forecast increases in demand.

- Impacts on the *quality of service* as a result of rapid increases in capacity to meet demands. This could result from bringing inadequately tested production facilities on-line resulting in increased product defects or scrap or through the use of untrained temporary staff brought in to cover peak demand periods.

- The ability of operations to be *flexible* in responding to unexpected increases in demand and to continue to *provide resilient services* during these periods.

- The simultaneous *availability* of resources. It is insufficient to have 99.9 per cent of the capacity available if the effect of a bottleneck caused by a small element costing pennies could prevent an entire process from operating. This is particularly relevant where operational capacity is fully utilized or where uninterrupted services are desired.

Capacity planning strategy

An organization's strategy for capacity planning will be influenced by the *market segment* in which the organization operates and the extent to which individual functions co-operate in developing capacity planning models for their individual business processes.

Effective capacity management should be linked with effective demand management. Strategic decisions regarding demand and capacity management are made using information provided by measuring current capacity and forecasting demand. Performance or capacity problems may be addressed by both designing and implementing increased capacity or by managing demand so that existing capacity is used more effectively.

Case study: Cleaning up the blockages

A manufacturing plant in Europe was not able to meet customer demand and the board needed to know how many additional presses would be needed to provide sufficient manufacturing capacity.

An operational study of the plant showed that shop floor workers took two to four hours to clean the presses between job batches and that as a result, on average the presses were only operating for 82 per cent of the time in any working week.

The study also showed that many customers of the plant had started to employ 'just-in-time' ordering strategies. The impact of this on the sales order process was that most customer orders were for relatively small batches.

The study concluded that manufacturing capacity could be increased by 11 per cent – which would be enough to satisfy expected customer demand in the medium term – by encouraging customers to place orders for larger batches. The increased productivity levels that were subsequently achieved offset the cost of volume discounts. No additional presses were obtained at that time.

Developing a capacity plan

In the event of a bottleneck or a process failure, a normal response among managers and operating staff is immediately to search for clues as to the source of failure. Typical areas for investigation might include:

- work-in-progress levels;
- lost items;
- the frequency of mistakes;
- the availability of machines;
- asking the following questions:
  - 'How many days of work-in-progress inventory are there?'
  - 'How many man-hours per unit are required?'
  - 'How often does the customer-request date match the actual delivery date?'
  - 'What is the ratio of the time the product is actually being processed to the total throughput time?'

In complex operations, however, a more thorough and systematic risk management approach is needed which considers a range of factors such as the market environment of an organization, strategy, tolerance for risk-taking among managers, and so on.

The key steps in developing an effective capacity plan may include:

Stage 1: Carry out a business process capacity planning health check

A business process capacity planning health check is carried out to assess the status of capacity and demand planning across the organization. The health check should be structured to ensure that the following questions are answered:

- Are existing capacity and demand planning processes effective?
- Would an increase in capacity lead to a significant increase in performance or output?
- Would changes to the current business processes result in better delivery results?

- Should existing capacity be upgraded or additional units installed?

- Would existing capacity meet the organization's forecast growth demands?

- Are there any technological developments, new processes, services, tools or other items available to change the capacity economically?

Stage 2: Analyse the current environment

At this stage, an understanding of the current environment including transaction or production demand is developed. This forms the basis for developing the capacity model in the next stage and includes:

- Understanding the existing capacity planning processes and their links to business objectives such as planned growth, new business initiatives and the business change process.

- Determining workload characteristics and resource constraints in current processes, such as the peak periods each month when a sales management information system is used by regional sales managers to download information.

- Understanding service level commitments. These are typically stated in terms of throughput, availability as a percentage of total time, rates or failure per day. These should be linked to business objectives since cost tends to increase at an exponential rate as service level targets tend towards 100 per cent.

- Identifying the key measurement criteria to monitor demand, including such measures as transaction rates, throughput, bottleneck analysis, response times error or defect rates. This should include identifying trends on an hourly, daily, weekly, monthly, quarterly, seasonal or yearly basis.

- Documenting the existing resources and costs allocated to the process including staff skills and training, business systems capacity and quality, machine asset utilization and bottlenecks, and physical space available for growth.

- Implementing tools to record and report demand and predict future (model) demand.

- Building a database to record appropriate capacity utilization measurement information develop reports to measure and report historical trends.

- Determining the timeliness and accuracy of management information to determine capacity planning strategy. This includes monitoring external influences such as market demand, competitor activity and initiatives, and economic influences.

Stage 3: Develop a capacity planning model

Based on the Stage 2 results, a capacity-planning model is developed. The development process should include the following tasks:

- Determining the short, medium and long-range capacity requirements against planned business objectives in the organization's business strategy.

- Evaluating alternative methods of building additional capacity to meet peak demand and growth, e.g. for size and location of production line or use of switched bandwidth to augment fixed bandwidth in a telecommunications network.

- Preparing detailed capacity planning designs and budgets that meet business requirements.

- Evaluating competitor activity and estimating an organization's current and likely future market share.

- Translating business growth estimates into the capacity requirements of each critical business process enabler. This may include hiring additional staff and training, new equipment or upgrades to existing equipment, or redesigning existing processes.

- Establishing the strategy for growing and reducing capacity to more flexibly meet changes in demand to ensure that fixed costs and capacity under-utilization are minimized.

- Identifying and mapping the cost increases related to capacity changes including staff, overtime and fixed costs.

- Developing risk assessment processes designed to ensure that future workload or orders can be accepted without impacting existing operational resilience.

- Building long-term relationships with suppliers and business partners to ensure flexibility of supply and services.

- Implementing analytical tools for capacity planning including break-even analysis, cash-flow analysis, simulation and decision tree analysis which determine payback and probability estimates.

- Developing benchmarks for comparing the performance of existing processes with other similar processes, business units or competitors.

Stage 4: *Management reporting processes*

The ability to measure and report capacity within an organization is a prerequisite for the effective management of both demand and capacity. Management reporting processes bring together information regarding demand and capacity from different sources. The information should be derived from historical, actual and forecast data sources.

Manufacturing and capacity planning

Managers increasingly recognize that manufacturing capabilities contribute to an organization's overall strategic strength and success. Capacity planning has a key role to play. For example:

- the ability to respond quickly to customer orders; the ability to customize products to match customers' exact requirements; and

- ramping up production rapidly.

However, many managers do not have the management information system needed to exploit fully their manufacturing capabilities. Managers confront a number of problems in this area, including:

- how to marshal the flow of work through a facility; how to translate customers' demands into products and services as quickly as possible; and

- how to involve operators in process improvements.

As well as the operating environment, questions need to be asked about the plant's strategic function:

- What does this plant aim to do exceptionally well?

- Does it aim for low cost?

- Or high quality?

- Or quick response?

Having a strategy often means focusing on one thing only. For example, large diversified paper companies may have two types of facilities. Those that produce large orders of low-cost commodity goods and those that produce small orders of high-margin speciality value-added goods with short lead times. Each type of operation requires a different plant configuration and different skills and practices. What is the highest priority? Cost, flexibility or quality?

In the context of adding new capacity to meet a rise in demand, managers often have to assess whether a plant can supply parts to another operation that may be developing new products. An argument in favour of choosing one particular plant over another may be a new investment in technology. At the same time, other systems may be too rigid to accommodate new products; floor space may be limited; and policies that made sense for long runs of comparatively stable products may collapse in the face of a rapidly changing production schedule.

Encouraging staff to think about operations

Organizations in declining industries often need to consider broadening their product lines. However, plant workers may have limited knowledge of the manufacturing process. They may know how manufacturing processes work but not why. Employees should be encouraged to ask questions such as:

- Why use this particular material? and

- How can the manufacturing processes be applied for making new products?

Availability is the degree to which an operational process is ready to work. An operation is not available if it has either failed or is being repaired following failure.

Availability may be measured in terms of:

- planned outages; and

- unplanned outages.

The causes of outages can be described under a few broad categories as shown below:

- **Environment:** Unplanned facilities failures may affect machine rooms, cooling external power, data communication lines, weather, earthquakes, fires, floods, acts of war and sabotage. Planned environmental changes may be needed to upgrade or relocate facilities.

- **Operations:** All the procedures and activities of normal system administration, system configuration and system operation. Unplanned outages are caused by operator or user errors and, rarely, by deliberate acts.

- **Maintenance:** All the procedures and activities performed to maintain and repair the hardware and facilities. Not all maintenance leads to planned outages, and a lack of effective maintenance can lead to unplanned outages. This does not include software maintenance, which is categorized under software.

- **Hardware:** The physical devices, exclusive of environmental support (air conditioning and utilities).

- **Software:** The software elements of a system including microcode, operating systems, operating subsystems, utility programs, application programs, software packages and network management software. Planned outages may be required to upgrade or repair software. Unplanned outages may result from software failures.

- **Data:** A lack of integrity in the data elements of a system including operating system control tables, databases, archived data, application programs, software packages and network definition tables may be the cause of unplanned outages. Planned outages related to data may be needed when upgrades or changes to data structure definitions are needed.

- **People:** Unplanned outages may arise as the result of the direct actions of people. Examples are labour disputes (strikes), shutdowns due to administrative decisions (stock exchanges shutdown at panic) and so on.

The categories of causes should be based on common sense and where appropriate, a pragmatic approach used.

An organization's tolerance to both planned and unplanned outages will vary depending on the nature of individual processes. As the need for a zero outage tolerance (planned and unplanned) increases, additional effort should be made to ensure that potential causes of outages are identified and covered by contingency measures.

Reliability

Reliability measures the ability of a process, system, product or service to meet an organization's operational performance

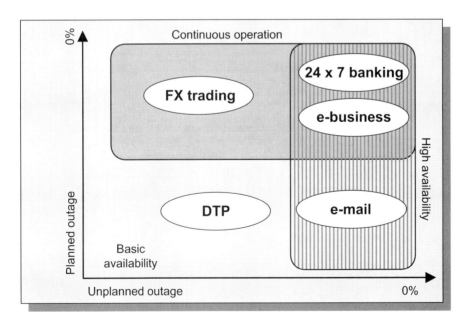

Figure 3.5 Different tolerances to both planned and unplanned outages

requirements. The components of reliability will vary according to those requirements, but may include:

- availability;

- performance;

- flexibility;

- confidentiality; and

- integrity.

The importance of any given reliability failure is determined partly by the effect it has on the performance of the whole operation or process. This in turn depends upon the way in which the component elements of the operation that are liable to failure are related.

If the components in a process are all interdependent, a failure in any individual component will cause the whole operation or process to fail to meet defined business goals and objectives. For example, if an interdependent system has n components each with their own reliability coefficient R_1, R_2, R_3 ... R_n, the reliability of the process as a whole, R_p, is given by:

$$R_p = R_1 \times R_2 \times R_3 \ldots R_n$$

where R is a number between 0 and 1, and:

R_1 = reliability of component 1
R_2 = reliability of component 2
etc.

Case study: Travel office

A corporate travel office within a large organization provides a wide range of travel-related services to professional staff. The ticket booking services provided have five major components, with individual reliability coefficients (the probability of the component not failing) as follows:

Process enabler	Reliability coefficient
Clerical staff	0.95
Telephones	0.99
PC workstation	0.97
LAN/WAN connection	0.90
Airline booking system	0.98

If one of these components fails, the whole process will stop working or fail to meet defined objectives. Thus, the reliability of the whole ticket booking process is:

$$R_p = 0.95 \times 0.99 \times 0.97 \times 0.90 \times 0.98 = 0.805$$

In this example, the reliability of the ticket process as a whole is 0.805, which is lower than the reliability of any of its components. If the number of components had been higher, the reliability of the process would have been even lower.

Redundancy

Building in redundancy in an operation means having counter-measures in place that minimize the impact of a failure. Redundancy (or recovery management) means doubling or tripling some of the process enablers so that these 'redundant' elements can come into action when one enabler fails.

The reliability of a component and its back-up is given by the sum of the reliability of the original enabler and the likelihood that the back-up component will both be needed and be working:

$$R_{a+b} = R_a + (R_b \times P \text{ (failure)})$$

Where:

R_{a+b}	= reliability of component a with its back-up component b
R_a	= reliability of a alone.
R_b	= reliability of component b.
P (failure)	= the probability that component a will fail and therefore component b will be needed.

Case study: Travel office (2)

The travel office in the earlier worked example has decided that the LAN/WAN link has become so unreliable that a second LAN/WAN gateway be installed so that it is activated whenever the primary gateway fails.

The two LAN/WAN gateways working together have a combined reliability coefficient of:

$$0.9 + (0.9 \times (1 - 0.9)) = 0.99$$

The impact of this change on the reliability of the ticket booking process as a whole is shown below:

	Clerical Staff	Phone System	PC Work Station	LAN/ WAN link	Airline Booking System	Total Resilience
Component reliability	0.95	0.99	0.97	0.90	0.98	0.805
Component failure reliability	0.05	0.01	0.03	0.10	0.02	
Contingency reliability				0.90		
Actual reliability	0.95	0.99	0.97	0.99	0.98	0.885

The financial impact of installing the additional LAN/WAN gateway may be assessed by examining:

- sources of revenue and relationship with process failure;

- impact on revenue generation of process failures;

- time taken to invoke recovery mechanisms; and

- cost of additional LAN/WAN gateway.

Case study: Travel office (3)

A sample profit and loss account for the ticket office used in the previous example is shown below.

Profit/loss account – assuming no failures

			Margins
Turnover	$11,550,000.00		
Cost of sales:	$11,307,450.00		
Gross profit		$242,550.00	2.1%
Expenses:			
Staff	$80,000.00		
Infrastructure	$40,000.00		
		$120,000.00	
Net profit		$122,550.00	1.1%

Assuming a 220-day year, an analysis of these accounts shows that on an average day thirty-five tickets are sold, with an average value of $1500. The information provided by the reliability analysis shows that the impact of process failures would have an adverse impact on the level of service provided. This in turn would have an adverse impact on turnover.

Without additional back-up measures (costing $15,000, amortised over three years):

Total non-operating time = 220 ¥ (1 – 0.805) = 42.2 days

The impact of a process failure is shown in the P/L account below:

Profit/loss account – operational failures/no back-up measures

			Margins
Turnover	$9,297,750.00		
Cost of sales:	$9,102,497.00		
Gross profit		$195,252.75	2.1%
Expenses:			
Staff	$80,000.00		
Infrastructure	$40,000.00		
		$120,000.00	
Net profit		$75,252.75	0.8%

With additional back-up measures:

Total non-operating time = 220 × (1 − 0.885) = 25.3 days

The impact of the additional cost of the back-up measure and improved process reliability coefficient is shown in the updated P/L account below:

Profit/loss account operational failures/with back-up measures

			Margins
Turnover	$10,221,750.00		
Cost of sales:	$10,007,093.25		
Gross profit		$214,656.75	2.1%
Expenses:			
Staff	$80,000.00		
Infrastructure	$45,000.00		
		$125,000.00	
Net profit		$89,656.75	0.9%

The additional cost of the back-up LAN/WAN gateway is offset by increased turnover because of the overall improvement in process reliability. The investment of $15,000 (over three years) is rewarded by a 0.1 per cent increase in the net profit margin and an increase in net profit from $75,252.75 to $89,656.75.

Failure rate

The failure rate (*FR*) is calculated as the number of failures over a period of time. For example, the failure rate of a generator engine can be measured in terms of the number of failures divided by its operating time:

$$FR = \frac{\text{Number of failures}}{\text{Operating time}}$$

Example:

50 generators were tested over a period of 2000 hours. Four engine failures occurred during the test as follows:

Failure 1 occurred at 1200 hours
Failure 2 occurred at 1450 hours
Failure 3 occurred at 1720 hours
Failure 4 occurred at 1905 hours

$$\text{Failure rate (as a percentage)} = \frac{\text{number of failures} \times 100}{\text{operating time (hours)}} = \frac{4 \times 100}{50} = 8\%$$

The total time of the test = 50 × 2000 = 100,000 component hours.

But:

one generator was not operating 2000 − 1200 = 800 hours
one generator was not operating 2000 − 1450 = 550 hours
one generator was not operating 2000 − 1720 = 280 hours
one generator was not operating 2000 − 1905 = 95 hours

Thus:

Total non-operating time = 1725 hours

Operating time = Total time − Non-operating time = 100000 − 1725 = 98275 hours

$$\text{Failure rate (in time)} = \frac{\text{number of failures}}{\text{operating time}} = \frac{4}{98275} = 0.000041$$

Mean time to failure

A common measure of failures is the mean time to failure (MTTF) of an enabler. MTTF is the reciprocal of the failure rate (in time). Thus:

$$\text{MTTF} = \frac{\text{Operating hours}}{\text{Number of failures}}$$

Example:

Given the failure rate of 0.000041 generated in the example shown above, then:

$$\text{MTTF} = \frac{1}{0.000041} = 24{,}390.24 \text{ hours}$$

That is, a failure can be expected every 24,390.24 hours on average.

Mean time to first failure

The mean time to failure calculation above may be used for a single component. In most complex environments, the time between the failure of a single component in a group of components is an important factor to be considered. If a complex system has three components, and the mean time between failure of each is MTTF1, MTTF2, and MTTF3 respectively. The mean time to the first component failure (MTFF) is calculated using:

$$\frac{1}{(1/\text{MTTF1} + 1/\text{MTTF2} + 1/\text{MTTF3})} = \text{MTFF}$$

> **Case study: Manufacturing plant**
>
> A manufacturing plant has a production line with three machines. The manufacturers provided details of the mean time to failure for each machine as follows:
>
> Machine A = 24,500 hours
> Machine B = 17,500 hours
> Machine C = 2,100 hours
>
> $$\text{MTFF} = \frac{1}{(1/24500) + (1/17500) + (1/2100)} = 1742 \text{ hours}$$

Human resource management

Introduction

With a strong emphasis on tools, techniques and methodologies to quantify risk, risk management methods have long approached risk from a purely technical perspective. While managing risk in this way undoubtedly provides advantages over previous, passive or reactive approaches, there is a danger that risk management practices can become one-sided. Too strong a focus on quantification, control and 'auditable' measures can mean that managers are not aware enough of issues and problems that are people-related. In reality, issues such as employee motivation and morale, attitudes and aspirations, management style and leadership, and approaches to problem solving and decision making, can have a massive bearing on how effectively risk is managed. Such factors are often ignored because they are less easy to quantify, but, ironically, may be more immediately known about. For example, low morale among staff is often very apparent but is unlikely to be factored into any appraisal of the success or failure of a business project.

Selected people/organizational predictors of project success

- Consistency in developing people and culture necessary to support changing business needs.
- Balancing the focus on technology or legal issues with an appropriate focus on organizational culture and change management.
- Ensuring that investment is made early on in addressing people/organizational factors.
- Balancing the pursuit of both quantitative and qualitative benefits.
- Instilling a performance mentality in staff demonstrated through their behaviour.
- Linking reward of staff to operational outcomes.
- Designing jobs to support performance-based compensation.
- Senior management sponsorship.
- Conflict resolution.
- Effective recruitment management and interpersonal techniques.
- Priority given throughout to cultural and people concerns.
- Estimating correctly the depth of change management needed.
- Appropriately assessing the role of people/organizational factors in relation to other relevant factors affecting performance.
- Overcoming destructive politics.

Approaches to risk analysis in conventional project management provide an illustration of the neglect of people-related issues. Typically, there is much excitement about IT and particular software tools to analyse risk. While these can be very useful in arming managers with decision-making tools, in reality, the reason for the success or failure of projects is often people-related. Upon reflection, most project managers will concede that the success of a project relies upon good team work, high motivation and co-operation, the minimization of conflict and the ability to address many of the factors featured in the box on page 134.

There is clear evidence to suggest that people/organizational factors do detract from conventional risk management approaches such as the creation and maintenance of a risk management framework. One recent study found that, where frameworks fail to be implemented effectively in an organization, the symptoms of that failure relate more to 'people/organizational issues' than tools, methodologies and other 'technical' risk management factors.

The neglect of people-related factors can be seen in the area of loss control and corporate employer liability insurance buying. This illustrates the close interplay between attitudinal and behavioural factors and conventional pragmatic risk management. Here, the focus has been the examination of company loss histories where risks have led to property/casualty and liability insurance claims, or, particularly in the US, workers' compensation claims. One issue that companies have examined in this way is that of incidence of back injuries, the largest single cause of absenteeism at work.

To mitigate risk, organizations, in conjunction with the insurance industry, resort to accepted risk management practices and put in place mitigating procedures, such as better manual handling training or ergonomically designed offices and furniture layout. However, evidence has shown that absenteeism for back injuries cannot be explained with reference to these factors. There are a range of other apparently non-related factors that tend to push people into having time off work when back injuries occur. These include job satisfaction, peer group pressure, job design, perceived stress and the degree to which employees feel in control at work. In other words, there are a range of psychological and behavioural factors that need to be considered when approaching loss reduction. Moreover, while running in parallel, these factors are independent of the scope of many organizations' 'traditional' risk management practices. Such factors may not be related at all to whether companies have 'traditional' risk management practices.

Finally, a similar pattern is forthcoming in the area of crisis management and business continuity planning (BCP). Often, people are only considered at the post-event stage, for example in the area of stress counselling. People-related factors are often ignored in planning for crises, such as how well will certain people respond, and is it worth allocating more responsibilities to those people who are likely to respond more effectively? It is obvious that issues such as effective communication, motivation and performance management all play key roles in effective BCP. Yet attention is often focused almost exclusively on the restoration of business IT facilities.

Case study: European retailer

A European retailer wanted to establish a shared services centre (SSC), which necessitated a redesign of internal management systems and the migration of processes into one centre. A number of people/organizational risk issues arose. These included:

- the redesign of jobs;

- a reduction in headcount;

- employing extra supervisory management staff; and re-skilling.

A key risk that had to be managed was that the environment of the SSC proved to be more dynamic than the normal environment and culture of the firm. This meant employing more proactive staff, prone to take the initiative rather than accept instructions.

Case study: UK retail financial services business

A financial service provider had achieved rapid growth over a seven-year period through successful direct selling of financial products. However, it had poor awareness of regulatory and compliance issues. In particular, information for customers to redress following the sale of a product was not adequately clear. Although its people were hard working and sincere, there was room for improvement in areas such as quality of sales, staff recruitment and assessment, and training. Closer analysis revealed a number of poor practices related to role models and leadership for sales procedures. The solution was a top-down, bottom-up review and assessment of skills and abilities. This was followed by a redesign of training programmes and competence assessment.

Case study: An overseas mining company

This global company had initiated a number of long-term, heavy-investment projects but was finding that it was experiencing poor motivation of staff. This was surprising, given that job security for staff was comparatively higher than companies in other sectors. In particular, there were a number of expatriate staff who were experiencing difficulties in managing operations and had complaints about compensation. This started out as a low-level risk but eventually proved to be threatening to the continuity of various projects. This dissatisfaction with compensation packages began to be resolved when a job redesign programme was instituted within the company.

Concluding points

- The recurring evidence points to the need to integrate people/organizational (P/O) risk management into the traditional operational risk management approaches.

- There has been an historical failure to do so. There exists significant advantages for businesses that adopt sensible techniques.

- P/O sources of risk are introduced into all forms of operational risk management such as BCP, business projects and business process redesign.

- Addressing P/O risks does not sit comfortably with managers because they can seem subjective and not amenable to simple measurement or manipulation, unlike other technical risks.

- Techniques exist to integrate P/O risks into conventional risk management in order to give them greater emphasis or focus.

- Such risks often do not emerge naturally. Therefore, they require proactive attention and facilitation to make them 'visible'.

- A failure to identify, diagnose, and address P/O risks creates a bow wave of latent risks which directly impact the quality of otherwise effective solutions.

- The treatment of P/O risks may require some specialist input as many factors are not easy to spot and some may serve to counter management initiatives. For example, they may have to be addressed by unconventional techniques.

- The reasons for ineffective operational risk management responses exist in a failure to tackle the underlying root causes that sustain poor risk management cultures. Often, that failure lies at the very heart of an organization's inability to make difficult decisions that in turn causes major problems, or at least prevents major problems from being identified and resolved at an early stage.

Supplier management

Introduction

Over the course of the 1990s, the once-neglected area of the supply chain has become a critical management issue that has led to the massive increase in investment seen in enterprise resource planning (ERP) systems seen in many industries over the last five years. Many organizations have analysed the process of moving goods between points to meet a level of customer service, and realized the scope to speed up product movement, cut costs, and remove waste and efficiency latent in the supply chain. As the case studies below demonstrate, operational risk management has an important role to play in facilitating supply chain efficiency and improving service delivery to the customer.

Rising interest in supply chain management partly reflects the changing structure of economies and markets. In countries such as the US and the UK, energies that were once put into manufacturing products are being displaced into the supply chain. For example, in the UK, manufacturing has long been in decline, leading businesses to export from overseas. Similarly, the expansion of, and removal of, barriers to markets around the world has given businesses more choice in sourcing supplies. These trends have necessitated a process of integration between, say, manufacturers and retailers, allowing businesses to achieve greater economies of scale, concentrate purchasing power and control prices, cut costs and improve the quality of customer service. Once restricted to economies such as the US and Japan, this process is now being repeated in the pan-European context, as markets there become increasingly more integrated.

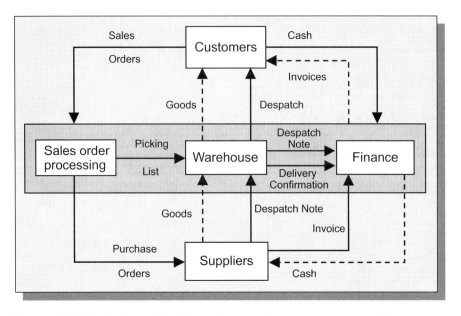

Figure 3.6 Typical supplier/manufacturer/customer process flow

In turn, organizations now require a more sophisticated system of co-ordination and control in the supply chain. The practice of logistics has been revolutionized in recent years by the use of electronic tracking systems, for example, that enable businesses and customers to track the precise movement of goods around the world.

Related is the drive to 'compress' order-to-delivery lead times. Businesses are finding that, with the revolution in production continuing apace in the world economy, competitive differentiation has shifted to speed and quality of customer service rather than the production of products that may become commoditized at a much earlier stage than in the past. The extent to which they can innovate in delivering a service, therefore, is crucial. Customer satisfaction – essentially the avoidance of frustration – has become a number one priority. Placing an order, therefore, should be as easy as possible for customers, and promises should be kept on shipment and delivery times. If a customer wants knowledge on the whereabouts of a product in the supply chain, or the order status, shipment or invoice details, businesses are now aiming to provide that information as instantly as possible.

For the same reason that businesses are shying away from long-term, fixed investment, they are finding that high inventory volumes tie up working capital and can work against the principle of satisfying customer needs. A major car manufacturer, for example, re-engineered their supply chain, with the result that cars in the supply chain pipeline represented four to five weeks' worth of sales, down from about six months of sales three years earlier.

With an increase in the number of products that hit retailers' shelves every year, product obsolescence – shrinking product life cycles – has become a real issue for many businesses. This is especially acute in the area of dynamic sectors such as information technology, where a particular model of personal computer can become out of date in a matter of a few months. This is often the main rationale for re-engineering supply chains. Nearly all major corporations have reduced warehouses and stocking points, and reduced the number of suppliers they work with, and final products are customized as far down the supply chain as possible in warehouses known as 'postponement centres'. Similarly, the greater interest in supply chain management mirrors the greater interest in conducting business from the perspective of processes, in order to improve customer satisfaction, which more closely match market principles and work across fixed, organizational departments and functions.

Case study: A UK luxury goods retailer

Entrepreneurial, high-growth organizations in sectors where customers are more demanding than elsewhere are often hindered by inadequate control over the supply chain. One UK retailer who imported high-quality fashion accessories from China, was faced with a number of risks in this area. Exposure to risk was further increased when the company decided to reposition itself from selling mass market, commodity items, to entering the premium, high-value fashion accessories market. This changed the risk profile of the company: the rewards were potentially greater but so were the risks. For example, after moving to a high-value market, customer demands on the company became more intense and its margin for error in product delivery was drastically reduced. This necessitated, in turn, a fresh examination of the supply chain with a view to reducing exposure to risk.

One problem was that knowledge of the supplier base was concentrated in only two company managers. This exposed the company to operational risk if those two individuals were to leave the company or could not be contacted. Similarly, only one individual – the managing director – was responsible for purchasing for the entire enterprise.

One risk management response was to create a detailed listing of the supplier base, assess the different capabilities of suppliers, and formalize a number of contracts with suppliers – up until that point most agreements were predicated on trust rather than legal contracts. Knowledge of the supplier base was formalized while at the same time making it accessible to many more members within the organization.

Geographically, the organization had a very long supply chain from China, which made supply chain control a crucial issue. The operational risk management solution was to put in place a better system of monitoring. A degree of monitoring took place but on an ad hoc basis. A new approach was elaborated which meant that products could be tracked at every key stage in the chain. The business then had a much better overview of where its goods were. A related issue was the degree to which stock was held up in the system. This would often be determined by the method of transport used. Items coming in by sea would take too long, but the wrong use of airfreight would increase the risk of an overstocking problem and the tying-up of more working capital than necessary.

A general principle that served to manage operational risk was 'formalize the informal'. One issue that arises with a smaller, high-growth company, however, is the risk of creating too much stifling bureaucracy by over-formalization. Often, the creation of contingencies, systems and hedges for everything in fast-growing businesses can stifle the very culture that made the company successful in the first place. The key was to achieve an appropriate degree of risk management while retaining an entre-preneurial, dynamic and fluid culture.

Case study: A US floral firm

A major US floral firm acquired a company in Holland to expand its market share in the supply of cut flowers. This was an acquisition of what appeared to be one company, but was actually four separate companies that were not integrated. As a result, each had individual distribution networks in their supply chains. There were inefficiencies in their downstream distribu-tions and there was a low awareness of costs. There was no single financial controller and an assessment of the costs of truck and van distribution networks revealed much higher than expected costs. There was also a lack of awareness of human resource management; in particular how training of personnel in the supply chain could lead to efficiency gains.

An absence of co-ordination and oversight in the supply chain often means that organizations sometimes spend far too much capital on distribution activities. In this case, on the upstream side, flowers were brought in by air from America, but the organization did not have an adequate idea of their spending on carriage, even though it was a multi-million pound operation. Again, one of the problems was a lack of co-ordination between individuals in the group.

One solution involved 'route optimization', involving an analysis of the supply chain focusing on a range of factors such as fuel consumption, vehicle times, the hours that can be driven, and human resource issues. Another involves reassessing strategic objectives. For instance, if spending on logistics is greater than 50 per cent, an organization may find that effectively, it is in a different business altogether.

Demand management was a key risk management issue. At special times of the year when demand increased for the floral firm – such as Valentine's Day – there was little knowledge of the lessons of previous years. The reason was chiefly an absence of data: little was recorded about historical demand patterns. At the other end of the capacity-planning spectrum, analysis of the supply chain highlighted inefficiencies that were not costed. Trucks, for example, would often carry out one-way deliveries, returning empty.

Risk management of potential supply chain alliances was also an issue. On the one hand, alliances present a number of opportunities: organizations can share information, which makes for efficiency gains, and can gain increased purchasing power. Joint training and transfer of personnel and the sharing of beneficial business practices can increase the knowledge base of each party. The downside is the risk of divorce at a time when both businesses may have become too important to each other to risk breaking up the alliance. In dynamic markets, such alliances can often be a liability rather than an asset. Building in flexibility is a key issue. There is a crucial balance to be struck: absolute trust is naïve, but at the same time relationships cannot be overly regimented.

Service management

Introduction

The difference between success and failure in today's business environment is often dependent on organizations achieving and maintaining 'best in class' service delivery levels with processes that are more reliable, less costly, more efficient or better than those of competitors.

At an operational level, the management of processes – particularly those supporting e-business initiatives – that meet or exceed demanding strategic objectives and operational service level requirements involves a number of core activities:

- planning and maintenance;
- defining performance measurement processes;
- setting and monitoring operational buffers;
- establishing operational back-up and recovery arrangements;
- preparing and implementing operational contingency facilities; and
- managing external communications.

Each of these activities is examined in more detail in the following paragraphs.

Planning and maintenance

The design, build and maintenance of processes should be a structured process subject to strict project management disciplines that ensure that every aspect of the process has been evaluated and its potential weaknesses identified and addressed. The design and maintenance process should ensure that process change is managed to maximize the speed of transformation with minimal impact on service delivery levels.

Defining the performance measurement process

Today, most organizations have far too many performance measures. However, in most cases these measures generally do not include measurements relevant to the management of operational resilience. To ensure the development of a relevant and useful performance measurement system, some basic design principles must be followed. Performance measures should be selected by establishing a clear view of the organization's business goals and operational performance requirements, by determining the objectives of operational resilience performance monitoring processes and by developing a strategy that will lead to their successful implementation.

Setting and monitoring operational buffers

Performance management and capacity planning techniques are used to set and monitor the operational buffers needed to provide sufficient capacity to process increased volumes or volatility in transaction rates and unplanned changes to business requirements. Buffers may be required for any operational process enabler and may include:

- using agency staff;
- reserve facilities and equipment;
- spare capacity;
- reserve computer and network processing capacity; and
- workflow and workload management techniques.

Establishing operational back-up and recovery arrangements

Action is taken to ensure that operational process enablers have appropriate back-up and recovery arrangements to prevent or minimize the adverse impact of failures. The nature of such failures is likely to cover those that have an adverse impact on process resilience (e.g. loss of operation of bar-code readers at a supermarket), rather than a catastrophic effect (e.g. an earthquake or flood).

Preparing and implementing operational contingency facilities

Contingency measures are designed and implemented to address catastrophic failures that may have a significant impact on the operational processes (e.g. a prolonged power loss or a major physical disaster).

Managing stakeholder communications

Steps should be taken to manage corporate communication aspects of:

- issue and crisis management;
- public relations;
- community relations;
- legislative and regulatory affairs;
- financial communication;
- media management;
- employee relations; and
- management, communication and marketing training.

Information technology

Introduction

IT facilities have become central to most organizations' operations. When computer systems go down for any significant length of time, businesses quickly lose their capability to compete in the market and customer service levels are affected. Over the past few years, most major corporations around the world have massively increased their investment in IT. In the US, for example, IT investment is thought to make up nearly half of all capital expenditure. In order to optimize investment in IT, organizations need to think about an effective IT risk management strategy.

There are a number of major areas that IT risk management may cover:

- mission-critical networks;
- process dependencies;
- digital business and information security; and
- disaster recovery.

Mission-critical networks

As telecommunications and new media continue to converge, organizations are making increasing use of corporate IP (Internet protocol) networks. Many organizations now have their own VPNs (virtual private networks), for example.

An IP network is analogous to using a telephone network: in a telephone network the complex task of running the service from the back office is handled by the infrastructure providers while the user devices – for example, telephones – represent a consistent user-friendly interface. The Internet is now seen as a means to an end, rather than an end in itself. For example, corporations are now using the Internet to increase co-ordination in the supply chain, penetrate new markets and build a stronger front office capability.

Making the most of these opportunities, however, depends in large part on how organizations can manage risk. There is a range of operational support issues. For example, like users of the telephone, users of the Internet expect instant connection to the network. However, at present, the same high levels of service and availability as telephone networks do not apply to IP networks, although there is improvement.

Process dependencies

Business processes are increasingly dependent on technology. This holds true in most industries. Technology is obviously most critical in areas such as air traffic control systems, nuclear power and public infrastructure organizations such as telecommunications firms. However, as organizations come under increasing pressure to perform, there are important operational risk matters to consider.

IT infrastructure may be categorized as the following:

- the application of technology to business processes;

- the linking of people and data through communications networks; and

- the way technology is used to manage the workplace.

In the past few years, organizations have focused attention on their IT infrastructures because they have sought to increase the synergies between their various business units. Through this, organizations have become process-oriented rather than business-unit focused. Technology has increased the opportunities to switch to a process-orientation, but there have been a number of associated risks. Organizations have to consider the impact of:

- unreliable or faulty hardware;

- major computer failures or crashes; and

- software viruses or other failures.

Digital business and information security

Electronic commerce – or e-business – has become a boom area. The use of electronic storefronts; the increase in on-line information services; the use of electronic procurement and transaction processing; the use of electronic financial services such as cash management and bill payment; and the use of intranets for human resource management; these are just some of the applications of this new technology.

Organizations face the risk of information security breaches.

In a recent survey by PwC, nearly three-quarters of respondents identified such a breach happening to them in the previous year. Organizations conducting electronic business were especially at risk – 59 per cent of respondents selling through their web-sites reported at least one security breach. Many could not tell if they had lost revenue as a result of security breaches. The arrival of a promoted British Standard for information security management (BS 7799) in 1995, which defined ten key risk controls, pushed the issue up the agenda of most corporate boards. But in many cases, a risk management strategy for monitoring and assessing information risk, and the damage it causes, is lacking.

Organizations need to feel secure and safe that they are certain of the identity of those with whom they are carrying out electronic commerce. They require assurances that the risk of fraud has been minimized and that business is conducted with confidentiality.

One way in which this issue is being addressed is through digital signatures – a series of electronic codes attached to the message by the sender. The recipient of the message can then check the signature and establish verification. Digital signatures require the use of certification authorities (CAs). These are institutions that go under the name of trusted third parties (TTPs). They can issue digital certificates that create the trust needed in transactions.

The use of digital signatures is already commonplace in the banking world, in the areas of Internet banking and discount brokerage. Gradually, an infrastructure is being created which is known as a public key infrastructure (PKI).

Organizations need to consider how to incorporate PKI into their overall infrastructure. Beforehand, they will need to consider how electronic commerce can be integrated with their business processes.

Disaster recovery

Business continuity strategy in the past few years has become increasingly sophisticated. In the recent past, disaster recovery tended to mean replacing IT equipment after a crisis. However, the focus today is examining how technology matters to the business, rather than estimating the replacement value of equipment, important as that is. Using this information, crisis managers can begin to anticipate recovering the links between servers, PCs, local area networks, and links between companies, their suppliers, and customers in the event of a disaster.

In planning for a failure of IT systems, IT needs to be considered in its broadest scope. For a start, IT encompasses a range of other equipment, such as telephones, desks, chairs and so on which may not be factored in to contingency plans. Similarly, systems require the use of skilled workers who, because of a crisis, may be out of operation. Third, computers may still be operational after a crisis but data loss may occur. Banks that lose only a day's data, for example, lose their trading positions and will be totally out of sync with their market.

Many businesses rely on computer systems to deliver their core product to market, exclusively so in many cases. These organizations tend to have built their reputation on having a faster channel to market than their competitors. As a result, these have to meet a far tighter deadline in terms of business recovery. At the same time, they have to consider how options for business recovery are narrowed: staff cannot be sent home, for instance and relocation to another site needs to take place much quicker. In an e-business environment, there may be no option other than to ensure continuous operations.

The purpose of disaster recovery and business continuity planning (BCP) is to minimize the operational and financial impact arising from any disruption to normal business operations. Effective planning is essential to minimize the impact of such disruptions.

Risk assessment addresses questions such as:

- What are the critical business processes within an organization's departments?

- What are the key IT systems that support them?

- What are the major threats facing the continuity of these systems?

- What preventative and contingency measures should be implemented?

- How should departments best develop a co-ordinated business continuity strategy?

A recommended recovery strategy may include:

- Provide a single supplier to co-ordinate together with recovery team relocation to temporary premises.

- Consider the ongoing workload needed to maintain the recovery plan.

- Test regularly the recovery plan, for both IT and business areas.

- Limit involvement of IT staff, who will be required to carry out other important support activities during this phase and plan longer-term recovery activities.

- Meet legislative and business requirements.

The provision of information and advice about business processes is key to making an effective start on the assessment.

Business continuity planning

Business continuity planning involves the following:

- business impact analysis;

- catering for large and small disasters;

- planning for long-term and short-term recovery;

- constructing target recovery timetables;

- allocating minimum recovery resources;

- establishing back-up strategies; and

- selecting recovery locations.

Business impact analysis

The purpose of this stage is to, first, determine which key processes and operational support facilities must be recovered, and, second, estimate the time-scale in which recovery must take place. This will involve:

- analysing the business to identify and prioritize the processes and dependencies in each part of an organization;

- prioritizing business processes according to their importance in an organization's department;

- identifying the critical dependencies on IT facilities and key personnel in each department which support the primary processes;

- identifying the threats to which the critical processes and enablers are exposed, and assessing the likelihood of threat occurrence;

- determining the likely impact of these threats on operational continuity and the probable recovery time-scale for each department to avoid serious disruption; and

- determining the adequacy of countermeasures in place to reduce the likelihood and impact of these threats, and recommending new countermeasures to enhance current risk management.

Large and small disasters

A business continuity plan needs to both cater for the possibility of ultimate loss of resources and more common occurrences of minor disasters. A fault on a server used by a small department may not justify the transfer of operations to the recovery centre, but it would require a recovery facility to reinstate the server within a short time-span on site.

Long-term and short-term recovery

Establishing a comprehensive recovery centre may take one or two years. In the meantime, however, businesses need to cover the risk they may be exposed to. As a result, business continuity strategies need to cover the short- as well as the long-run scenarios.

Target recovery timetables

As part of the evaluation of critical business processes, it is necessary to consider the maximum time an organization can be without each business process before the effects of disaster are felt – for example, the maximum time before a business process must be restored. These are defined as the target recovery time-scales.

Minimum recovery resources

Each computer-based business process has a number of resource requirements that need to be calculated. Essential resources required during operations under recovery conditions need to be identified. There are two distinct phases involved in recovery from a business disruption:

● the preparation of the recovery site(s) – for example the recovery operation itself; and

- the operation of critical and necessary business processes under recovery conditions once the recovery site(s) have been prepared for use at the completion of the recovery operation.

Related to this concept of two distinct phases of recovery are two sets of teams involved in recovery from a business disruption:

- the teams that conduct the recovery operations are designated as disaster recovery teams; and

- the teams that conduct the operation of critical and necessary business processes under recovery conditions are designated as critical department teams.

For each critical and necessary computer-based process, there are a number of requirements to be considered including:

- software;

- networks and communications;

- supplies;

- vital records, including computer based data;

- equipment, including configuration and transport;

- personnel, including the functions that each completes;

- transport required for each resource;

- utilities;

- office/industrial space; and

- suppliers related to each requirement.

The majority of this information may be documented within the organization, in procedural manuals and so on. However, existing information may be not readily available or may be outdated.

Back-up strategies

The key to a successful recovery of business operations is dependent on having adequate copies of relevant and secure data, computer programs and documentation. Regardless of how sophisticated the current recovery programme is, if the organization cannot reconstruct its data and operating environments at the time of the disaster, recovery will fail.

The importance of back-ups has only recently been realized. The increased reliance on computer systems for information recording, results in an increased exposure to significant financial loss if back-ups are not made because of the amount and value of the information held. Many organizations would collapse if their information technology operations were disrupted for a week or more, while others are even less tolerant. This has meant that infrequent back-ups stored on-site are no longer sufficient.

The selection of a back-up strategy incorporates the issues of in-house and off-site storage, back-up frequency, number of back-ups required, archiving, responsibility for back-ups and maintaining adequate documentation to make use of back-ups.

Recovery locations

Locations for assembly of personnel, control of recovery operations and processing under recovery conditions need to be identified, evaluated and selected. A disaster can be of any scope, and may be classified as a unit, local or regional disaster. For each type of disaster site, primary and alternate recovery locations need to be identified.

The primary recovery locations should be suitable for operations in the event of a local disaster of large proportions, where another site is required to continue processing. The alternate sites should be for regional and unit disasters. The selection of the type of recovery site will be influenced by the maximum downtime for business processes and the cost of the recovery site facilities.

Suitable assembly locations should be identified where personnel can meet at the time of a disaster, to enable the safety of personnel to be assessed and to determine the initial recovery actions. An assembly location should be close to the original facility. A recovery must be controlled, including the set-up and use of the recovery sites. Therefore, a separate command centre location should be established from which the recovery operations could be directed. The user recovery site must have appropriate services and enough space to permit completion of recovery tasks and must be available for a sufficient length of time to permit the return to normal operations in the original or a new location to be completed. The best chance of speedy recovery is for the primary user recovery site to be customized to suit the organization's requirements and maintained in readiness for occupation. In a unit disaster, it may be possible to use the original site, perhaps on another floor.

Where mainframe computing is involved in the critical and necessary operation of the business, special environmental requirements must be considered. The options for computer recovery sites involving mainframe-computing facilities are typically classified into hot sites, cold or shell sites. These are supported by mobile sites, reciprocal agreements and arrangements with service bureaux.

- **Hot site:** immediate recovery to a duplicate data centre, within twenty-four hours.

- **Warm site:** recovery to a third-party recovery services provider, within five days.

- **Cold site:** recovery to a 'shell' computer room on premises, or portable computer room, within thirty days.

Warm site options represent a low risk option for recovery of IT facilities since detailed recovery plans can be developed and regularly tested. There may be difficulties locating suitable areas for mobile warm recovery services.

Cold site options are likely to be less expensive than warm site options. However, these would not permit detailed IT recovery plans to be tested. There is also a risk that computer equipment may not be available at the time of disaster.

Where there are distinct computer and user recovery sites, the recovery of communications is extremely important for the resumption of computer-based processing.

Case study: The effect of smoke

A national library had a fire in its roof. The computer room was two floors below. The fire did not affect the computer room until the fire brigade arrived, when the computer room doors were opened, allowing the smoke-laden air to enter and causing immense damage to disks.

Case study: Learning from the past

A bank suffered bomb attacks in the City of London. The bank lost its offices in the first bomb and as a result decided to formalize a plan. This took the form of an agreement with another bank to use their recovery site in east London. The planning process was undertaken and was completed on a Friday (although it was yet to be tested). The very next day, the second City bomb went off and wrecked their offices again. This time they had a plan that swung into operation. The bank was trading from the recovery site on the Monday morning. This goes to show the importance of business continuity planning and that catastrophes can and do happen twice.

In the event of a large-scale business disruption where the facility has to be repaired or a new facility found, it might be necessary to select more than one recovery strategy. Separate recovery strategies may be required – for example, one strategy for the immediate restart of operations and another for interim processing prior to relocation to a permanent site. The selection of strategies will depend on time limits at the recovery site(s), their cost and the time required to prepare a facility for normal operations. In this phase, the different requirements of each location are assessed, suitable locations identified and final locations selected.

Case study: The consequence of complacency

A head crash on an old disk pack set a halon gas fire retardant system off in the computer suite of an organization.

There was an opportunity to override the discharge of halon but the organization had a propensity to test the alarm system at irregular intervals and at odd times of the day. The alarm went off, but everyone ignored it. The halon was discharged and the people in the computer suite panicked and fled, believing that being in the room with the halon would kill or seriously harm them. They required extensive counselling afterwards.

Because of environmental concerns, the halon was not recharged until agreement was reached on a plan to replace it as a fire retardant. The day the new gas was eventually delivered (four weeks after the discharge) was a Friday and it was decided to leave it until the following Monday to reconnect the gas. That night there was a fire in the computer suite as a result of arcing on a loose 100-amp earth connection that dropped molten metal onto a pile of old printed circuit boards left on the floor. The building was filled with acrid smoke and the fire brigade was called, but at first they could not find the source of the fire.

After about two hours, they found the fire and with a quick burst from a hand-held extinguisher, put the fire out. The fire was located directly beneath a halon discharge nozzle.

The disaster recovery plan went into full swing and about two days' processing was lost. The major damage was from acid formed by the reaction of the smoke with moisture in the air. Nearly all the telecommunications equipment had to be replaced, but the computers survived.

A month later (on Boxing Day), the building's uninterruptable power supply (UPS) apparently damaged by the result of the arcing, literally blew up leaving the computer suite without power. The computers were down until the UPS was repaired.

Sourcing management

Introduction

Outsourcing refers to the transfer of the management of a corporate function or process to a third-party vendor. It has become a major business trend in recent years. Some of the most popular functions currently outsourced include IT, human resources, finance, administration and separate business processes particular to an organization.

Outsourcing poses a number of critical operational risk issues. Simply put, the operational change it necessitates, involving human resources, physical assets, business processes, technology and so on, can bring about new operational risk exposures that require extra management oversight. The risk profile of an organization – the different mix of risks and their possible impacts on it – can be altered in the process of outsourcing.

Many outsourcing arrangements are high risk, high reward projects where the potential pitfalls are huge. Outsourcing brings about uncertainty. A new relationship between supplier and corporate customer represents an untested agreement. No one can be absolutely certain that the function or process will be run more efficiently or with the same standards as it was managed in-house. A key part of risk management is taking the time necessary to carefully define business objectives in measurable terms, structure contracts that link vendor performance to the realization of those objectives, and actively manage relationships in order to ensure those goals are sustainable.

Although different forms of outsourcing pose different kinds of risks – some more substantial than others, depending on the criticality of the function or process being outsourced – all involve operational risks that require careful management if the outsourcing process is to achieve business objectives. A holistic approach to outsourcing, one that evaluates both the risks and rewards, is crucial. For example, some organizations enter into outsourcing from the standpoint of reducing risks. They may outsource functions where it may be difficult to find highly skilled workers in the labour market – IT being an example. An organization, however, would fail to benefit from this strategy if it was not managing other operational risk exposures adequately. Or, through poor management, it may increase its risk exposure in other, undetected areas.

The objective of outsourcing should be to free up management and instil confidence in them to take on more risk in the core areas of the business which are most adding value. Rather than fearing a loss of power and control when functions or processes are outsourced, management should feel comfortable and be confident enough to use outsourcing as a platform for achieving key business objectives. Ultimately, the aim of risk management is to ensure risks do not threaten existing business strengths.

Central to achieving stability over the course of the outsourcing agreement is managing people. Managing expectations and conflict involved with people can take more time and resources than managing the change-over in processes. Jobs are often at stake in an outsourcing agreement and more senior managers may feel uncomfortable with change. They may feel they are being demoted if, for example, they suffer a loss of control over key staff. Ensuring that staff morale is high is an integral part of making an outsourcing project successful.

A sound business case can help to mitigate much of the operational risk by providing direction and certainty in working towards defined goals. Many businesses approach outsourcing from the perspective of attempting to outsource an operational problem that they would rather not deal with, especially in areas such as IT. Organizations have to understand why they want to outsource, what they want to outsource, who they want to partner with, and how contractual agreements with third-party outsourcers should be defined. A point that needs to be constantly stressed is that whatever vendors do for an organization, in the eyes of customers and shareholders, the organization is ultimately responsible for the results. Organizations cannot achieve their goals simply by shifting responsibilities onto a vendor. This holds true in the case of a huge deal to outsource a whole department or business process, or contract with a vendor for more modest services. In either case, organizations must use techniques such as negotiating benchmarks and incentives with the vendor as part of the contract process and assigning enough managers to oversee projects effectively.

Conducting a feasibility study is often vital. In the case of IT, this may examine the organization's existing technology infrastructure and application development, with a secondary focus on the identification of selected business processes that may be outsourced.

The evolution of outsourcing

To understand the operational risks posed by outsourcing, it is necessary to understand its shifting strategic importance. Outsourcing is beginning to represent a major organizational change in facilitating a new way of conducting business. It reverses the historical tendency for organizations to create and develop in-house functions, as instead control of these functions is increasingly being transferred to third parties.

The outsourcing of computer operations or data centres to vendors has been one of the most common forms of outsourcing. Organizations have been able to cut costs, as vendors have been able to achieve economies of scale. In many cases, there have been benefits of having a specialist pay attention to the issue of technological obsolescence – ensuring that an organization's technological facilities are up to date and best able to support the organization's strategic goals.

The future of outsourcing lies not in outsourcing IT departments but in outsourcing business processes (BPO). This promises to deliver a number of opportunities and benefits to customers, but will also increase operational risk, sometimes quite profoundly.

Initially, the types of activity that were outsourced by organizations tended to be peripheral to operations, such as catering or payroll processing. As a result, the outsourcing process posed minimal risk in terms of business disruption or operational discontinuity. The motivation for outsourcing tended to be tactical, often as a cost cutting exercise.

Today, outsourcing is seen from a different starting point. Organizations increasingly take a strategic rather than tactical perspective of what it can achieve.

The context is:

● Increasing competitive pressures due to globalization. Businesses are being outperformed by competitors in increasing areas of their business that they are not specialists in. As a result, they have examined where they have market-leading capabilities and shed those parts of their businesses that are lowering overall efficiency.

- The potential for technology to create more efficient business processes, which has resulted in the realization that organizations have to change their own business processes to remain competitive.

- The pressure on managers to increase performance, profit growth and shareholder value. Management everywhere is under pressure to optimize the use of the resources at their disposal. In today's context, under-utilized capital, people, technology and so on risks the accusation of poor management and the possibility that managers will be replaced by dissatisfied shareholders. In many cases, this has led to a greater willingness to change among senior management and a willingness to reengineer business processes.

- Enterprises have more options than ever before in creating structures for their vendor relationships, such as value-based contracting and multi-vendor outsourcing deals.

Some of the main reasons that organizations consider outsourcing include:

- the reduction and control of operating costs;

- improving organization focus;

- gaining access to world-class capabilities;

- freeing internal resources for other purposes;

- accelerating reengineering benefits;

- improving management control;

- making capital funds available;

- helping minimize share price risk;

- avoiding being swamped with extra administration during a period of growth; and

- minimizing need to accelerate a learning curve in a new business area, or conversely, to cut the need for investment and to avoid placing the quality and efficiency of an existing outsourcing service at risk.

Probably the most significant driver of outsourcing is the relatively new tendency for companies to focus on core competencies. More organizations are thinking ahead and enquiring how they can acquire core competencies, at what price, in what time-scale, in order to compete successfully in the future. Many have established chief resource officers to oversee change and outsourcing. This is in tandem with the trend for businesses to organize around their most efficient processes where they add most value, rather than tasks. In particular, they are strengthening the efficiency of those business processes involved with their core competencies.

Outsourcing risks exposure

The use of outsourcing as a strategic management tool, however, also increases operational risk in a number of ways.

- Although outsourcing is becoming more strategic, the most basic problem is a lack of strategic clarity before outsourcing takes place, and/or a failure to take into consideration strategic change in the future, which might change the nature of the outsourcing relationship.

- Some outsourcing transactions are now worth billions

of pounds, with success or failure making a greater difference to an organization's overall financial position and reputation in the marketplace.

- As outsourcing involves the handing of control over to a third party to run a function or process, there is always the risk of initial business disruption. Similarly, this risk also occurs at the termination of the contract when there is either contract renewal or the function or process is handed back to the control of the customer.

- Organizations become newly dependent on third parties to manage what could be a significant part of their operations.

- Increasingly, in the economy more generally because of outsourcing, corporate resources are lying outside the corporate sphere. This is adding to a massive value of contracts and services which necessitates a stringent management of the risks and rewards.

- If the strategic aims of an organization change, there is the risk that service contracts become outdated and inflexible.

- Although outsourcing generally suggests a more efficient way of doing things, the customer may find that the outsourcing vendor is not more efficient in running a function for them.

- The service responsibilities of the outsourcer and retention of responsibilities by the customer may be ill-defined, leading to disputes later on.

- The management of the customer may resist because they fear a loss of control or that what they are good at is being displaced to a third party.

- The outsourcing vendor may fail adequately to understand their customer's business, which increases risk for the customer. Outsourcers need to take a strategic perspective of the customer's vision, current and future core competencies, where it adds value, positioning in the market, and so on.

- In the case of outsourcing the IT functions, there may be an increased risk of access to private and sensitive data.

- In the case of outsourcing of human resources, organizations are transferring over what is one of their most significant assets.

- Staff oppose the outsourcing because of a reluctance to change.

- Organizations have to anticipate a dip in service delivery as soon as the third party runs the outsourced function for the first time, since brand new processes are immediately engaged and during this time, uncertainty is high. Live tests (in the area of network stability, for example) cannot often be carried out prior to running the function, so there is a need to expect the unexpected.

Key challenges involved with outsourcing

If organizations are able to exploit business opportunities through outsourcing their functions and perhaps using them as a critical business enabler, they may have to consider the following (using IT as an example), prior to outsourcing:

- Reengineer and simplify processes to a common standard.

- Create a common systems platform that is implemented the same way everywhere.

- Implement business partnering between IT and the business units globally.

- Identify and develop alternative outsourcing solutions for enhanced IT service delivery.

- Improve and align the service levels and responsiveness of the IT organization to business needs.

- Align IT costs to meet business/financial objectives.

- Implement change programmes and effective project management.

- Establish a single point of contact for service delivery.

Human resource management

More specific risks occur when dealing with particular outsourcing models. For example, organizations are outsourcing human resource management to third parties for several reasons including:

- to allow a third party responsibility for the administration of hiring new employees;

- to transfer responsibility for ensuring compliance with new employment and workplace regulations particularly in a multinational environment; and

- to centralize the management of employee benefits.

The extent to which organizations reap these benefits depends on their success in managing risk. For instance, organizations are paying more attention to their 'human capital' and are keen to retain those staff which they consider valuable, or have valuable knowledge. Human resources itself has become a more highly valued function and is considered more from a strategic perspective. Outsourcing vendors become newly responsible for managing this human capital which is critical to the success of the organization overall.

Secondly, the question of liability – important to all outsourcing arrangements – may be especially important in the case of human resource management outsourcing. An important consideration is that outsourcing contracts (see later) rarely transfer liability to the vendor; the customer is often still liable to its employees for the actions of the vendor. This puts the onus on the customer to manage risk carefully. It means that organizations have to maintain a high degree of management oversight and supervision to ensure that they are compliant and aware of regulations and standards. Where practical, the use of independent third parties to monitor the performance of outsourcing service providers should be considered.

Business process outsourcing (BPO)

BPO promises to be the future of outsourcing. It involves both the outsourcing and redesign of business processes.

The context for its development is that large organizations need to innovate and stay ahead of the competition. They also need to act swiftly to complete new projects, such as a new product launch. However, internal bureaucracies and sheer size, as well as cultural factors such as risk-aversion, may prevent organizations from acting quickly enough to take advantage of market opportunities.

For example, an organization may research a new market but realize that the window of opportunity to be first to launch a new product is six months. However, with too much internal bureaucracy and a slow decision-making process, it may be too slow to move that fast. At the same time, it may not have the specialist resources for product design and appropriate changes to IT systems. Outsourcing the process to third-party specialists can achieve the objective of launching the product.

Another common area of BPO is winning and retaining customers, with the help of speedier and more efficient business processes. An example lies in financial services when customers apply for new credit or banking, or insurance policies.

A screening process that takes a number of weeks is likely to result in potential customers finding they want to go elsewhere. Through reengineering and outsourcing, an organization may find it can halve that time. In the case of an insurance company, it would retain its core competency – that of underwriting – but may outsource the screening process to a third party which has more efficient processing tools and methodology, using cutting-edge IT systems.

Operational risks increase because businesses are placing more of their strategic objectives in the fate of others. The impact of risk may be that much higher.

Managing outsourcing risks

There are four key areas in which a focus on operational risk management can bring benefits during the planning stages of an outsourcing project:

- pre-outsourcing preparation;
- managing the contract;
- assessing the risk of subcontracting; and
- communicating the plan to outsource to the stakeholders involved in the outsourcing.

Pre-outsourcing preparation

One of the main, and basic, barriers to achieving success with an outsourcing contract is that management is not clear what it is trying to achieve in the first place. As a result of bad planning, it may rush into an arrangement without carrying out the adequate planning.

Some basic rules may include:

- Evaluate the experiences of other organizations that have outsourced.

- Position a key champion (this may be the chief resource officer) to oversee the planning and create an outsourcing team, with representatives from human resources, finance, law and operational managers.

- Assess the culture of the outsourcing vendor for signs of a cultural mismatch.

- Review vendor proposals.

- Evaluate the potential for a strategic partnership. This may be more appropriate in the case of BPO where a key element of the business is being outsourced. The benefits include a sharing of the risks and rewards. The downside could be that, in the context of a closer relationship, cultural differences stifle efficiency.

- Anticipating staff management. One of the major operational risk management considerations with outsourcing is people management. Any outsourcing arrangement involves a change in work for staff involved. This change may be welcomed or approached with reluctance by both the staff and management. For example, staff could interpret the move negatively, as an unwelcome career move. Management could fear losing some of their most trained and talented people.

Managing the contract

Negotiating and managing the contract in an outsourcing agreement is a major way in which customers can mitigate risk exposure. This is critical to the success of the outsourcing outcome. The contract provides the guidance for behaviour, responsibilities and roles that will be considered on a daily basis.

In managing operational risks, customers have to ensure that the contract embodies both certainty and flexibility. This can be quite a tricky balance. Not every unexpected event can be legislated for. At the same time, however, as with all contracts, parties want to avoid lack of clarity that could provoke disputes or disagreements. Such a scenario is likely to increase the possibilities of business disruption.

There are two related issues:

● avoiding over-legislating; and

● adapting to change.

Within the outsourcing arrangement, vendors will ideally take it upon themselves to offer value added services based on changing needs of their customers. A too prescriptive contract could define responsibilities too narrowly. This could prevent vendors from 'thinking out of the box'. They may be reluctant to introduce changes that could benefit the customer, at a time when innovation is required. Although innovation is not something that can be guaranteed, it is possible to stipulate that innovation is in the mutual best interest of both parties.

One of the major complaints with contracts as they stand at present is that they do not offer the required level of flexibility to cope with future change. This has been evident in the IT area. Here, businesses need to shift quickly to the use of new technologies so that they can increase the efficiency of business processes and increase competitiveness. IT contracts may have to be renegotiated, which may not prove the best way of doing things and pose the risk of business disruption.

In this sense some contracts have had an effect opposite to that which was intended, by stifling innovation and hampering businesses. The contract is the most important mechanism for freeing up businesses to innovate and adopt a more risk-taking approach. It is also where the relationship between outsourcer and vendor is defined. For example, some outsourcing arrangements, if sophisticated, facilitate a partnership approach where both parties share more equally in both the risks and rewards of the arrangement.

The responsibility of the contract should rest with the management of the customer rather than vendor. Contract management is usually necessary as an on-going process. This may include:

- managing changes to the contract;

- auditing the performance of the vendor to ensure that the terms of the contract are being upheld; and

- managing penalties and compensation.

One of the most common outsourcing risks is that the needs of the organization change to such an extent where the service being provided by the outsourcing vendor is no longer relevant to its business direction. As discussed above, this is becoming a more common possibility, as companies need to change their strategic positioning on a regular basis. The extent of operating costs may be higher than written in the contract and there may be friction between the parties.

Managing the termination

An important consideration, which is often overlooked, is that the end of the service requires careful risk management. In particular, there is a risk that, since the outsourcing vendor is at the end of the contract and potentially losing business, it will be less vigilant to the possibility of business disruption. Another risk is that organizations may not be able to terminate a contract, or at least, may do so but under conditions that encourage business disruption, rather than minimize it.

Monitoring performance

Outsourcing vendors are judged on performance. The contract specifies how that performance should be measured. The monitoring of performance can take place better through more sophisticated information management.

Components of the contract

An outsourcing contract is like any other, containing four main components:

- **Scope of work:** This section lays out the range of activities the outsourcing vendor will carry out for its customer. In the case of an IT contract, the scope of work may describe how the vendor constructs an IT system for some specific task, tests the system, and operates it for the purpose of the customer's business. In this last stage, the service level agreement of the contract will kick in.

The details in this section may include:

- any equipment bought by the vendor, hardware and software;

- details of maintenance;

- network specifications; and

- back-up plans for data and archiving facilities.

A costing and work plan is normally included.

Although each of these is critical in its own right, the majority of the problems that occur post-contract revolve around definitions laid out in the section the 'scope of work', which describes the roles and responsibilities of the outsourcing vendor. Here, differing interpretations of the text can lead to potential problems. Another problem is that omissions in this section could lead to one of the parties shouldering costs which later leads to a grievance.

Risk management considerations include:

- including enough detail for a record of initial plans, especially important if staff originally involved move on; and

- clarifying what is 'in scope' and 'out of scope' as this will be debated regularly in the context of on-going operations.

1 **Deliverables:** This details what the outsourcing vendor will provide, build and turn over to the customer.

2 **Terms and conditions:** This section will normally be the most text-intensive part of the contract, and will cover possibilities that will probably never occur, such as early termination of the contract.

3 **Service level agreement:** This details the services that are to be provided on an on-going basis. It will include details such as **volumes and response times** of a particular service. Often, the costing will be linked in, so that the greater amounts of processing, the more telephone calls answered, data used, and so on, can be charged to the customer.

Assessing the risk of subcontracting

One common reason why management feels uncomfortable with outsourcing, understandably, is the fear they will lose control over a key part of the business. This fear can then be confirmed if outsourcing firms further subcontract work to other parties. This 'double-outsourcing' often takes place when vendors need to use specialist skills, especially in the IT area, when they themselves lack expertise. On one level, this benefits the original customer, as they have access to a broader skill base. They have more resources to draw upon, and as a result, may find that they are in a better position to enact, and respond to, change.

On another level, potential operational risks have already been made apparent. For example, in an aerospace company outsourcing arrangement, a subcontracted employee temporarily disrupted its e-mail system through malicious behaviour.

The main risks of 'double outsourcing' include:

● Poor communication due to a widening chain of employees, and cultural differences. One organization may have a culture where sophisticated communication is normal, while another may not. This can lead to operational problems and sluggish response times.

- Viruses brought in by outsiders. This can be a common problem if service providers are in contact with a wide range of organizations. It has the potential to cause both a loss of reputation and business disruption.

- Unexpected costs and the possibility of low quality service which may not be detected for a longer period of time. This may be related to poor training in specialist areas, even if staff have the right skills.

According to International Data Corp, around a third of all subcontracting arrangements involve further subcontracting. Their vendors do not always inform management of the customer being serviced that 'double-outsourcing' is taking place. There is a range of risk management solutions to minimize these risks:

- Liability management can be included in the contract. This will protect the customer and ensure that the first contractor is legally responsible for possible failures or malicious behaviour of subcontractors.

- The use of contractors which only have a 'preferred status' by their vendors. This can reduce much of the time needed for risk assessment since enough information will be gathered on particular firms by the prime contractor.

- Extended interviews with employees to build up a historical view, when possible.

Communicating the plan

Once the decision to outsource has taken place, communicating the outsourcing plan to employees is a vital part of operational risk management. There are a number of considerations:

- involving the employees as soon as possible, perhaps with the use of employee forums; and

- communicating the implications for benefits, pay and career mobility in general.

Risk management outsourcing

Historically, success of the financial sector has been based on institutions being able to continue to develop, sell and deliver profitable financial products. The traditional role of risk management in the financial sector has been to help management understand the potential impact of:

- changes in business strategy;

- new products on the market;

- the market on both new and existing products;

- changes in economic conditions at local and global levels;

- changes in regulatory and legislatory conditions;

- operational failures; and

- accounting and transaction processing breakdowns.

Within many financial institutions there is limited central co-ordination of risk management and control activities. In a typical financial institution, individuals may be found working in a risk management capacity across the organization. The range of risk management job titles in a large institution may include:

- business risk management;

- market risk management;

- credit risk management;

- financial risk management;

- internal audit;

- operational risk management;

- fraud risk management;

- insurance risk management; and

- compliance risk management.

By outsourcing certain business processes, financial institutions can greatly improve the performance of those functions or departments as they support the overall business. The outsourced processes can be redesigned to achieve higher levels of productivity and efficiency – which translate into increased profitability. One of the other key benefits of outsourcing is that management can be freed up to focus more of their time and attention on building the institution's core business. Responsibility for managing the day-to-day operations and administrative activities is transferred to the outsourced service provider. The outsourcing of risk management processes is an area that until now has not been given a great deal of attention.

The key stages of a typical outsourcing project are shown in Figure 3.7.

Some of the most popular functions currently outsourced include finance and accounting, internal audit, tax compliance, human resource management, application processes, procurement and real estate management.

Risk management processes – other than internal audit – are in most institutions an integral element of their core business processes, and as a consequence, risk management outsourcing is not common. The outsourcing of the technology supporting risk management on the other hand is something that many institutions have considered and in some cases, have carried out.

Audit committees and management shoulder fiduciary respon-

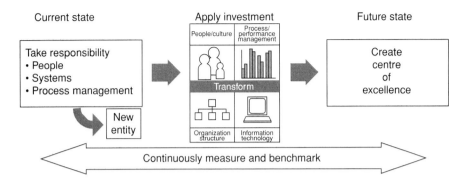

Figure 3.7 Key stages of a typical outsourcing project

sibilities for corporate governance. Internal audit professionals perform a top-down review of the company's associated business, operating, and financial risks – and strengthen controls to better manage those risks. The nature of internal auditing is such that it has to remain independent from an institution's core business processes. Consequently, this is one aspect of risk management in which process outsourcing is commonplace today.

Internal audit outsourcing may cover the management and execution of every aspect of internal auditing including: defining the role and responsibilities of internal audit, organization and staffing, scope of examinations, risk assessment, audit plans, work programmes, visitations, computer auditing, special projects, and reporting.

Project management

Introduction

Projects are the principal vehicle through which organizations of all types implement strategic and operational change. A project may mean the creation of a physical asset through investment, or refer to a wide variety of business changes, from a merger or acquisition to a new product launch. Many of today's projects involve the implementation of large, complex IT systems. Another typical example is a corporate relocation project, involving the relocation of staff, possible new recruitment in the new location, as well as a host of IT and data transfer issues.

Since projects are essentially creative and lead to new opportunities, and since the contemporary business climate places a high premium on continuous change, organizations are, today, more compelled to enter into a variety of projects on an ongoing basis. The fashion in which a project is managed can make all the difference between its success and failure. Moreover, the successful management of a project has become a key to how companies create competitive advantage overall.

The way in which people interact on a project and work effectively as a team is the most important single factor determining its probable success. More specifically, the effectiveness of teamwork between all project stakeholders is key. Project stakeholders typically include:

- the business management responsible for delivering the improved business performance that was the justification for the project;

- those responsible for delivering the new systems, structures, buildings, processes and so on necessary to achieve the improved performance;

- the 'targets of change', those people who will have to change the way they work or interact with the organization as a result of the project. If the project directly impacts customers, then this group includes the customers themselves; and

- senior management, whose support and guidance is almost always a major factor in ensuring that major projects are aligned with corporate strategy and receive the support necessary to deliver planned benefits.

Those projects most likely to succeed are those with cultures that are:

- open;
- constructively challenging;
- teamwork oriented;
- risk eliminating;
- goal directed;
- quality conscious;
- achievement recognizing; and
- service focused.

E-business projects need to be fast, meet key deadlines and deliver a high quality product if organizations are to beat the competition while avoiding some of the recent damaging headlines in the press over poor service quality. New ways of establishing and maintaining supplier relationships quickly are often key to achieving this. Both established and start-up clients have difficulty achieving these because:

- they do not have the expertise and methods or try to apply traditional techniques when greater flexibility is needed;
- they do not aggressively manage risk and remove uncertainty;
- poor project management often results in compression of essential activities to prove the solution works at each stage; and
- they establish inappropriate or inflexible supplier relationships and fail fully to integrate the supplier.

The importance of an open culture

Major projects are almost always strong learning or discovery experiences. At their beginning, there are huge uncertainties as to precisely where business performance needs to be improved, how this can best be done, what degree of flexibility needs to be built into the project, what has worked before and what new techniques and technology will prove to be reliable.

During the project, it is inevitable that some aspects of the work will run behind schedule or get into difficulties. It will also usually be the case that unexpected changes in the business environment occur that may impact some of the assumptions that underpinned the original business case or project plans.

Unless these facts are communicated accurately and quickly to all relevant parties, it becomes impossible for timely adjustments to be made in the whole programme of organizational change to accommodate them. Understandably, this can quickly lead to irritation and to an undermining of trust and teamwork.

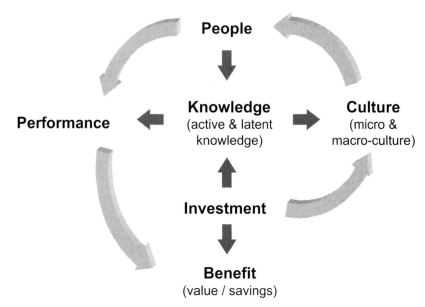

Figure 3.8 Cultural considerations

The health of a project depends upon a climate of openness in which facts and uncertainties are communicated quickly without inhibition. Three factors will generally determine how well this is done:

- the effectiveness of uncertainty management;

- the effectiveness of quality and progress control; and

- the reactions of others to bad news.

The effectiveness of uncertainty management

If residual uncertainties in costs, benefits and time-scales are not recognized and communicated, then it will be impossible to manage people's expectations. In the absence of information on uncertainties, there will be a tendency to assume certainty, that planned dates and budgets are firm, for example. In private, management may doubt that plans are achievable, but many will find it convenient not to have been informed officially that there are inevitable uncertainties surrounding plans. In some cases, this will enable them to blame others outside their area of responsibility when dates are missed. In other cases, it will enable them to put considerable pressure on the people who have committed to the dates or costs and to extract huge degrees of effort from them to achieve these.

In either circumstance, there will be great pressure on individuals who have not communicated information on inherent uncertainties to deliver to commitments. On the positive side, this may mean that they and their people work very hard. On the negative side, it means that it will become very difficult for them to communicate the fact that they are not going to deliver on their commitments. The management task is to remain sufficiently close to realize the true situation and make plans accordingly. Usually, however, senior management has to cope with a huge range of issues simultaneously and may not have any independent sources of information as to the true state of the project.

The effectiveness of quality and progress control

If quality and progress control is not effective, then people will simply not know if a project is overrunning, or building in expensive defects that will subsequently need to be corrected at large expense. When problems do eventually come to the fore, it will then become even more difficult to communicate them openly; doing so would require admitting that quality or progress control has been ineffective to date. While people may feel comfortable admitting that they underestimated effort or costs, the admission that expensive errors have occurred, or progress has not been tracked effectively, does not come easily.

The reactions of others to bad news

In an ambitious organization of ambitious individuals, it is quite common to find an aggressive response when somebody is accused of letting others down by failing to deliver to commitments. The attempt to avoid such a response, however, may lead individuals to delay or distort the communication of the true nature of the problem they have encountered on the project. This can seriously compound the problem. In the worst cases, there may be in effect a conspiracy to keep top management in the dark as long as possible about the true state of a project or the reasons for its delay.

Projects are far more likely to succeed if a climate is created where people are encouraged to communicate 'bad news' and be rewarded for doing so, provided that it is done constructively and accompanied by suggested solutions.

Achieving an open culture

Achieving an open culture is one of the most difficult challenges on any project, a goal hindered or supported by the existing culture of the organization as a whole.

Organizations may consider a number of techniques in achieving an open culture. These may include ensuring that all estimates of costs, benefits and time-scales at every level are done on a 'best probable' and 'worst probable' basis.

This is not the same as allowing for, or fixing in advance, contingencies to every task or estimate. Some estimates can be relatively precise because there is a well-documented and comparable history upon which to draw. In other cases, levels of uncertainty will be very high. In such cases, it is probably not a good idea to form a single 'most probable' estimate figure. Doing so suppresses the most useful piece of information that exists about that estimate – its uncertainty.

The process of managing uncertainty can only come from recording and communicating that uncertainty. If estimates are known to be uncertain, managers begin the process of achieving a better estimate, or alternatively allowing for the worst probable case scenario in the planning process. The worst probable case scenario will usually be unacceptable, given commercial constraints. But recognizing uncertainty in an estimate is not the same as failing to set challenging targets.

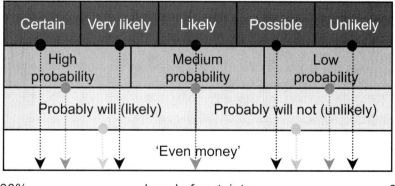

Figure 3.9 'Soft' uncertainty quantification tool

Employing an independent assurance team

A second measure that can promote an open culture is employing an independent assurance team with a remit to review all aspects of the project periodically, and report on any lack of realism in progress reports and plans. With an independent team conducting a review every two or three months, those working on the project will tend to realize that there is no point in suppressing the truth. The independent review team can also draw attention to any untested assumptions and uncertainties in the business case and project plans.

Develop a supportive culture

A third measure is to develop a supportive culture. This essentially means developing a number of principles or ideals that are strongly communicated by the project leadership from the start. These may include ensuring people acknowledge that:

- the project meets ambitious cost, benefit and time-scale targets. To achieve these, assumptions cannot be left untested, defects undetected or risks and concerns not communicated; and

- teams will earn respect because targets are tough. No criticism will accrue to people who make mistakes or overrun estimates for good reason. But failure to communicate known risks or problems, or failure to co-operate fully in the quality control and assurance processes will lead to trouble.

The importance of 'constructive challenge'

One of the main barriers to project success is a lack of 'constructive challenge', particularly in the early stages. People are under pressure to proceed with the project and meet early deadlines for analysis and planning. The issue, however, is that decisions regarding objectives, technology, design and planning, taken early on, have the greatest potential consequences. During the early stages of a project, it is generally much more important to expend time and effort to ensure that the objectives are right and are aligned with organizational strategy, the technology is robust, the benefits are achievable and that the plans deliver benefits as early as possible. It is also particularly important to ensure that a project can deliver the required benefits into all the probable scenarios that the organization might face. Flexibility should be prioritized in both solution design and in delivery planning.

Some of the key challenges and questions include:

- What have you done to satisfy yourselves that this is the best solution to delivering the required improvements in business performance?

- What other options exist and how have you made sure that all feasible ones have been identified?

- What proof do you have/do you plan to get that the planned return on investment is achievable?

- Why can't we improve performance more? What are the principal constraining factors?

- Why can't we deliver the project/benefits earlier/more cheaply? What are the principal constraining factors?

- What are the principal assumptions you have made regarding business direction, robustness of technology, productivity levels, etc. and what have you done/do you plan to do to test them?

- What processes have you been through/do you plan to go through to ensure that your answers are correct on all of the above questions?

- Who have you involved in these processes?

- What are our main competitors doing and what are their plans?

- What are the key risks and how do you plan to manage them?

This 'challenge process' should occur as frequently as possible during the early stages, in order to ensure that all options are fully investigated. An important point is that the challenge process should be good-humoured and constructive, rather than overly aggressive, which may inhibit presenters and reduce their ability to communicate arguments effectively. Once this information is suppressed, so usually are the actions necessary to reduce or manage this uncertainty.

Building teamwork orientation

The importance of effective teamwork across the organization cannot be over-estimated. Most major projects affect substantial numbers of people and require resources from many different quarters. Many major projects are learning experiences and comprise teams of people who have never worked together. As a result, a major requirement is a continuous flow of information between project stakeholders, as more is learned each week about the nature of the challenges faced. The flow of, and response to, information will be affected by the quality of relationships between the various stakeholders and how they perceive their priorities. A major task of management is to ensure that accountabilities, responsibilities, priorities and authorities are appropriately aligned in relation to each project deliverable. For example, if the production of a particular interim deliverable, such as a specification, requires a cross-organizational team to work together to tight deadlines, then it is essential that all the team members have a shared sense of urgency and that they all receive recognition and reward for producing the deliverable. The sense of responsibility that comes from a shared sense of urgency often prompts ideas and actions to reduce the risk of failure. This may be more difficult to achieve if the team members report through different lines, and have many other demands on their time.

Among the most important measures to ensure teamwork is effective are:

● promoting effective uncertainty management and constructive challenge (see above);

● ensuring that there is a powerful project steering group that is held jointly accountable by top management for the success of the project, and in particular, for providing the resources and the support needed by the project. The role of the project steering group should be to ensure the success of the project, not merely to monitor its performance. Ensuring that every single project deliverable (including improved business performance) and interim deliverable (including for example project resources), has clear delivery responsibilities, backed by a clear project plan and well defined standards for the end product, processes for producing it and quality control processes for accepting it; and

● putting in place a good process for regularly monitoring morale on the project and for addressing problem areas promptly.

The importance of 'goal direction'

One danger is that the original goals of a project can become forgotten among the minutiae of weekly events. Even project milestones can be expressed in terms that bear little resemblance to original objectives.

However important a project may be, it is often difficult for people to remain wholly focused on an event that may be a year or two away. To circumvent this problem and motivate the project team, a series of regularly occurring milestones is needed that each represents genuine achievement and progress towards the ultimate goal.

The best demonstration that a project is under control and is being properly planned and managed (subject to it having the right objectives and the right milestones) is its ability to hit its short-term milestones. If a project team cannot hit these using the information they have at their disposal about the nature of immediate tasks, their ability to meet longer-term milestones a year down the line will be thrown into doubt.

A milestone should be:

- sufficiently frequent to give prompt warnings of a project falling behind schedule if they are missed;

- meaningful at board level, being expressed in terms that they can readily understand;

- expressed in terms that demonstrate real progress towards the overall goal, drawing in as many work-streams as possible;

- expressed also in terms that demonstrate that the required quality of work has been achieved and that there is continuing strong confidence in the project; and

- as far as possible delivering direct business benefits or at least substantial value, even if subsequent stages of the project encounter problems.

Producing and signing off a business specification is not, by this definition, a goal-directed milestone. A goal directed milestone could produce a technical specification that has been walked through using a rigorous process and checked against pre-defined quality criteria aligned to the business objectives::

- by people who have the qualifications and experience to

identify any serious defects that could adversely affect the planned benefits or ROI;

- who have demonstrated their understanding of what they have reviewed; and

- who have committed to delivering at least the minimum business benefits currently envisaged as achievable from the implementation of the solution as described.

If it is economically feasible to break a project down into frequently occurring milestones, that each deliver business benefits directly, and that substantially reduce any residual uncertainties in the planned ROI from the overall programme or project, then this represents a particularly powerful form of goal-directed project planning.

Quality consciousness

Quality consciousness is a necessary attitude of mind in all-important projects. The right interpretation should not imply over-engineering or strict adherence to standards: both of these traits can undermine success on a project. Rather, quality consciousness refers to absolute focus on the quality needed to maximize return on investment and achieve the necessary move towards the organization's strategic objectives.

The nature of projects is that every stage of the work builds on work done previously. A project that fails to identify a defect quickly ends up investing more and more in that defect as the project progresses. At worst, a major defect introduced at the specification or design stage, and undetected until near the end of a project, can result in the scrapping of all a project's work. At best, it can result in major re-work, increasing costs and delaying the realization of the benefit stream for a protracted period.

A quality conscious culture is one that encourages:

- setting target quality attributes for every piece of work that represent the minimum necessary to achieve the project's overall objectives;

- creating plans and processes that enable this target quality to be achieved first time round; and

- checking quality frequently to ensure that the target quality attributes are being met, especially during the feasibility, specification and design stages.

Top level progress reports on business projects may contain little information on how the actual quality of project work compares with the planned quality, or on the amount of re-work being done. Achieving a strong degree of quality consciousness on projects is often best achieved by requesting that a quality plan be prepared which identifies, for every deliverable and interim deliverable:

- the target quality attributes (for example the minimum contents and level of detail of a new project plan, the required costs per transaction of a new business process or the required decision making speed of a new organizational structure);

- the planned process by which the requisite quality levels will be achieved first time and the responsibility for this;

- the quality control process and responsibilities; and

- how the results of the above will be reported in the top level project progress reports (e.g. by reporting defects found against target by producer and quality controller).

Achievement recognition

Business projects are usually about changing some aspects of the way people work. Most project teams usually comprise people who are able and hard-working, enjoy improving particular processes, in the context of working in a field where it is difficult to predict with any certainty cost and delivery times. Senior management is constantly seeking predictability of results, not least because this is what shareholders demand. In this environment, praise for project managers and their teams can often be in short supply.

This is a problem in itself, and can work against getting the most out of project teams. Project teams may have slaved away for weeks or months to meet a deadline that was never achievable. They may have acquired a reputation for failure by missing deadlines only very narrowly. The danger is that morale on such projects can sink to very low levels.

The view that if project teams are not set challenging targets against which they are likely to fail, they will not work as hard as they otherwise could, is often prevalent. The ideal environment is one where targets are recognized by all as being challenging, are generally met, with the result that a project team gains a reputation for being exceptional. There are of course no easy answers to achieving this. The following approaches can be of assistance:

● Set a wider range of performance measures that focus on the key drivers of project success that are relevant every day of the project. These should include as a minimum quality of planning, level of defects and track record of hitting short-term milestones.

● Set earliest and latest probable dates for the short-term milestones and lowest and highest probable costs and benefits, ensuring as far as possible that the worst probable outcomes reflect genuine uncertainties rather than possible productivity problems.

● Use an independent assurance team to review the project estimates and uncertainties and to recommend challenging but realistic targets; grading these according to what should constitute acceptable performance, what would be good and what would be excellent.

- Use an independent quality assurance team also to review and grade quality of planning and reliability of information flows on defect rates.

- Link rewards for project team members to their track record in achieving short-term milestones, maintaining good quality plans and achieving low defect rates.

Service focus

The final cultural characteristic that tends to be supportive of successful projects is closely related to teamwork orientation. The difference is that it applies to areas of the organization that may not have a major role to play in the project, and may not even consider themselves part of it.

Often, a project can be unnecessarily held up or even thoroughly demotivated by poor service from line departments or even from top management. A common cause is a demand from line departments of fixed estimates of resource requirements when these are inevitably uncertain, or if top management delay decisions on essential additional funding.

One answer on large projects or programmes is establishing separate procurement, finance or HR functions within the project under the joint control of the project director and relevant line department head. However, where this is considered impractical or counter-cultural, it is necessary to instil within the relevant line departments and top management a recognition that major projects do carry considerable uncertainties for much of their life and therefore often require excellent service at short notice from line functions. This should not of course be an excuse for poor planning or communications by the project team. As in all other areas, they should be capable of identifying requirements within ranges well ahead and refine these as time progresses. However, the line departments should be expected to treat projects as customers and respond with responsive service level agreements.

Risk management

One of the major problems with project risk management is that it is too easy to take the process of risk management seriously enough. Often, the perception is that risk management is carried out solely to please the internal audit function, or particular organization guidelines. This encourages a piecemeal approach: for example, it is common to find that some type of risk assessment is carried out, but it usually remains in the form of a passive list which remains sitting in a database not actively pursued. Even the basics of risk management are often overlooked. Project managers are usually very busy, dealing with sponsors, suppliers, making progress reports, and so on. Often, there is a need to define the role of the risk manager differently, so that they are not about avoiding risk *per se* but making processes work better.

Taking the next step involves designing a number of mitigating actions, and making a decision whether to retain particular risks. Risks need to be assigned ownership, and management action plans need to be built into the overall plan for the project. Risks then need to be tracked so that project sponsors know about the risk.

The key is aggressive management of the risk. This is more of a mindset than anything else, or an attempt to build a 'zero-risk culture'. It involves defining project goals in a new way. The objective is to factor in more contingencies with regard to the dates of project milestones and then to ask what are the uncertainties and assumptions involved with assuming that.

Project management is too often seen as an individual skill. In fact, it is an organizational competence. There needs to be a steering committee of members responsible for overseeing the project.

A related point is that risk evaluation can also be used to modify decisions in the bidding process; unhidden risks or opportunities may decrease or increase the value of a project and may have to be newly accounted for.

The second main point is that when considering risk management, risk should not be viewed too narrowly. The ultimate aim of risk management should be to cultivate confidence among managers to achieve more ambitious goals within their projects. Any project represents an act of risk-taking to enhance return, willingly entered into by its sponsors and organizers. Risk management should aim to provide more certainty about the possible risks that can have an impact on the project. Effectively, this then gives managers more options to take more risks to maximize return, should they need them.

An example of how this works in practice is that many projects are rejected because managers feel they do not overcome organization hurdle rates – the required rate of return on investment. In many cases, raising hurdle rates has become a proxy risk assessment procedure for large sections of industry. The problem is that first, this caution occurs in the absence of any objective analysis of probability and impact of risk; and second, many opportunities which may lead to profitable returns are discounted from the start. Overall, better risk evaluation can help management capitalize on opportunities that they would otherwise reject.

Another main reason risk assessment has become critical is that project sponsors, investors and other stakeholders increasingly need more assurances that projects will be completed on time, expected returns will follow, and in the process resources will be used as efficiently as possible.

Risk and impact

There are two key phrases at the heart of project risk management: probability and impact. It is important to make a distinction between the two. The probability of occurrence of risk is different to the impact it may have. Impact is the severity of the effect on the budget, project completion, or the project's ability to satisfy customer demand.

Keeping this distinction in mind, project risk may be categorized in the following way:

1 high probability, high impact;

2 low probability, high impact;

3 high probability, low impact; and

4 low probability, low impact.

Each risk requires a different level of management supervision. A combination of two methodologies may be applied: containment planning and contingency planning. Containment planning refers to what can be done to neutralize the risk. In some cases, nothing can be done – for example, there is little one can do to prevent natural disasters. Similarly, constraints imposed by regulation, perhaps indicating time deadlines for a project to be finished, cannot be wished away. Contingency planning refers to how operations and actions can be modified if a risk has a material impact on the project.

Each category requires a slightly different mix of the two methodologies. Category one requires the highest degree of containment and contingency planning. In effect, the risk has to be neutralized if possible, and the project has to be most prepared since the likely impact will be the greatest. Category two requires careful supervision, a lesser degree of containment but the same level of contingency planning. Category three requires more resources be put into containment but less into contingency. Category four arguably needs the least containment planning and least contingency planning. A key consideration is that risk exposures may change in the course of the project itself. This is itself a risk that needs to be taken into consideration.

Key risk areas

An effective way to break down project risk management is to categorise the likely threats into a number of distinct areas: inherent risk, financial risk, scheduling risk, external risk, implementation risk and technology risk.

Inherent risk

Some projects are inherently risky because of their nature. Inherently risky projects include those with a strategic importance, where success or failure could have material impact on financial results or on an organization's public image or reputation.

Inherent risks may also include the risks originating from intangible factors, such as:

- Is the organization's culture compatible with the goals of the project?

- Is the organization over-ambitious?

- Does the new project fit the core competencies of the organization?

This category also includes the risk of too many projects taking place at the same time. The root cause is often a lack of proper processes to approve various projects and allocate funds to them. Similarly, the same projects may take place in different geographical places, at the risk of creating more problems because of non-compatible systems. The starting point to solving such problems is for someone within an organization to have a strategic overview of the projects commencing.

Financial risk

    This includes asking questions such as:

- Has the budget won approval from key decision-makers?

- How much is being spent on the project?

- Have the financial benefits been quantified?

- Are they realistic?

Scheduling risk

    This includes questions such as:

- Is the time frame achievable?

- Are the resources and skills available to complete the project?

- Related to this, are there enough staff that can be freed from their normal day-to-day work to participate in the project?

- Are there too many projects happening simultaneously within the organization, competing for limited resources?

External risk

    These are the risks external to the organization. They may include the risk of failing to meet a regulatory requirement. This is an issue especially for financial services firms. For example, after the recent pensions mis-selling scandal in the UK, all major pensions providers were required to offer compensation and were set very challenging deadlines to sort through past records in order to do this. The Financial Services Authority was keen to monitor project plans. The reputation of financial firms was on the line as a spot-check could reveal poor plans and lead to negative publicity.

    Another example of an external risk arises in the outsourcing context and the managing of suppliers. Companies are increasingly critically dependent on IT suppliers. Often, organizations seem to trust their suppliers more than their own people, often because it seems as if contracts underpin and therefore safeguard outsourcing arrangements. As a result, organizations often neglect effectively to monitor their suppliers.

> **Case study: External risk for a financial services company**
>
> A financial services firm demutualized and had to acquire premises to administer shares and deal with enquiries from members of the public. Around ten million application forms had to be processed in just two weeks. While the technology side of things progressed relatively smoothly, with specialist machines to process forms, the biggest single risk to the project was on the human resources side.
>
> To address this risk, hundreds of temporary staff were hired from agencies. Given the limited extent of local travel and parking facilities, and the fact that local residents and travel companies would not co-operate, the issue of how those staff were going to get to the new premises was soon raised. The massive temporary increase in the size of the workforce at that location also raised health and safety concerns regarding sanitary and catering facilities.
>
> Temporary office accommodation, with sanitary facilities, was erected in a car park on site. An external catering firm was hired and a coach company from outside the area was contracted to transport temporary staff to the site. Overall, the project proved very successful because the risks were recognized and managed.

Implementation risks

This category is not exclusively focused on IT but covers any system that is part of the on-going business. Key risk issues include:

- Has there been adequate training of the user community?

- Are there help desks set up?

- Is the documentation there?

- If a new product is being launched, is the marketing tied in to the launch time?

Case study: Implementation risk for a bank

A bank decided to build and implement a call centre to allow consumers to buy a new financial product. The biggest risk was that the firm would get flooded with demand. A key strategy for managing this risk was to manage the way they marketed the product. For example, they adopted a stage approach, marketing initially to existing customers before beginning a poster campaign in their branches

---

Technology risk

This is especially relevant with the increasing pace of change of technology today, and the pace of arrival of new products on the market. In general, organizations can gain advantage by using new technology. Some risk issues, however, may include:

- Is the technology tried and tested?

- Is there an adequate skill base – can you find people who have used the technology before?

Crisis management

Introduction

Every year, businesses around the world are thrown into crisis because they suffer the impact of a severe, unexpected event. Many of these, such as shipping accidents, train crashes, chemical leaks, sudden financial collapses or terrorist attacks, hit the headlines and become high-profile disasters. For the management of these businesses, having a prepared plan to respond is critical and is likely to be the single most important factor in minimizing long-term damage to the organization. The right response is especially important today considering that organizations operate in a 'global goldfish bowl'; the globalization of news networks and advances in communication technology means that any disaster will soon become common knowledge around the world.

Crisis management has different drivers in different industries. In some, such as oil and gas, crises represent a very major and repetitive threat to normal activity. Here, management has become highly attuned to crisis management as a fact of life. In others, such as the financial services sector, crisis management as a subset of risk management has been driven more by regulation and recent upsets to global institutions caused by rogue traders, currency devaluations and economic upheavals. Crisis management will inevitably differ in strategy and implementation according to industry sector, and the particular significance of a crisis at a given time will depend partly on the nature of that industry.

Business continuity planning has been a management issue for at least the last twenty years. But crisis management should not be confused with disaster recovery, which refers more specifically to repairing immediate damage and returning business operations to normal as quickly as possible. As a management practice, it incorporates aspects of disaster recovery.

But it may be considered as a separate discipline in its own right. Effective crisis management is much more dependent on the right cultural factors being in place before a disaster strikes. This inevitably means it is more complex and hard to get right, compared to previous disciplines in this area.

A crisis is defined as such because it can bring an organization to a sudden halt, throwing short-term (and if severe enough, long-term) business survival into doubt. A crisis leads to a significant diversion of resources into areas other than normal business operations. Thousands of extra man-hours and resources are used up in order to contain the crisis and get the business back to normal. Extra pressure is placed on the switchboard, fax machines and computers. At the same time, businesses have to manage stakeholder reactions. It is normal for share price to fall post-disaster, and public confidence in an organization may be dented. New business opportunities are put at risk in times of crisis.

Crisis effects can have 'ripple events', either more widely within an organization and/or in the wider community. A fire at a plant, for example, may lead to unemployment and pollution, facilitating other kinds of crisis.

A crisis puts tangible and intangible assets at risk. The operational phase of a crisis usually receives the greatest risk management attention. A loss of tangible resources has usually already occurred. After that point, the organization's intangible assets are at risk, and the key is to minimize damage to market share, share price and other aspects of reputation. After the initial event causing the crisis, the organization involved is compelled to turn around its image in the marketplace and regain competitive edge. A crisis, being unexpected, leaves management with limited time in which to respond. Decisions need to be made quickly to limit further damage. Traditional hedges such as insurance have a very limited role to play – the key is a prepared, proactive and intelligent management response.

After a crisis, the business needs to be 're-normalized'. This refers to returning the structures, systems and people back to a functional state that is equal to, or better than, the environment that existed before the crisis. Formally called impact recovery management, this process may take years. If litigation for example follows a crisis, as is often the case, then uncertainty as to the full cost and damage to reputation of a disaster continues to prevail.

By its nature – dealing with an unexpected event at short notice – crisis management cannot be a full-time job and a crisis manager is not a full-time position. But crisis management is a necessary strategic investment, and its value is instantly realized when the unexpected occurs. Naturally, businesses are reluctant to make a large investment in something that offers no promised commercial return. As a consequence, emergency planning is often under-resourced. There is therefore a need for support for crisis management at the highest management level within an organization.

The scale of investment in a business continuity plan will also be contingent on the size and scope of the business. In a small organization, the investment may amount to no more than a proportion of the owner/manager's time. A larger business may appoint a full- or part-time business continuity manager, to contract with external service providers, or to invest in standby premises and facilities.

According to recent studies, 80 per cent of companies that do not have a workable crisis management plan will fail within one year of a major disaster taking place. Businesses are much more accustomed to planning against commercial risks – the failure of a critical supplier, an unforeseen bad debt, industrial action, or a serious production process malfunction as examples. The principles which they base risk management on, however, may be seen as applicable for crisis management. At their simplest level, risk management techniques in place in most organizations require an assessment to be made of the nature of the *threat*, the level of *risk* that will occur and the *consequences* of that risk for the business. This appreciates the vital distinction between probability of risk, which may be low or high, and the impact a risk has on a business, which can vary in its intensity.

It is clearly difficult for management to assess, and prioritize the management of, the impact of a crisis. There are some basic first steps that management can take, however. The first is to quantify how an organization might be at risk from a crisis, and visualize and construct a series of disaster scenarios. Management can assess the impact of wider political, economic and geographical risks, and research should indicate if prior crises have occurred in particular business localities. Local authorities may be able to reveal whether there is a real propensity for any given disaster in each location. This thought-process will allow management to begin to form a view on the potential downside of each crisis, based on an assessment of objective and subjective factors. For example, a crisis that impacts the organization from the outside may be exacerbated if particular organizational weak spots already exist and are activated in some way by the crisis. In addition, much of crisis management is identifying the cause and effect of risk, and the way in which different risks correlate which then increases the negative impact on an organization. For example, an airline may believe that – short of one of its planes actually crashing – a malfunctioning of its reservations system represents one of the most severe crises it could encounter in its operations. That view, however, may overlook the fact that its underlying maintenance system should be covered by a crisis management strategy, and that its reservations system will not be restored to normal operations without the proper working of the other system.

The second step is to nominate key personnel who will manage the fall-out from any given crisis. This necessarily involves a division of labour. People who understand particular branches of business and organization matters will be best placed to react promptly and effectively. The managing director, by contrast, will probably not be available to manage and oversee recovery processes immediately following a crisis, but could play a vital role at the level of public relations. The main point is that there must be a clear chain of command, and individuals require a clear awareness of where they stand in a crisis management team, whom they report to, and what their duties are consequent on any crisis event.

The third step is to identify the particular trigger mechanisms that initiate planned responses and procedures to a crisis. A prerequisite for this stage, and a successful crisis management strategy in general, is the free flow of information throughout an organization. Once triggers have been activated, information channels to management should be as open as possible. These communication channels must be robust, and their intention must be to circumvent the effects of a severe crisis becoming disruptive to a business. A thought-out management structure will increase an organization's chances of success in controlling the damage that follows a crisis.

Using crisis management to maximize business resilience

In the wake of the IRA terrorist bombing campaign in the UK, the Home Office published a guide 'Business as Usual'. This aimed to educate British business about maximizing its business resilience to the bombing threat. The lessons contained in it have a wider application and form the basis of the following analysis, which contains advice for dealing with three main stages of a crisis: incident, recovery and continuity.

It is unnecessary to develop separate plans to deal with separate types of risk that fall under the crisis umbrella. By focusing on the consequences of the crisis (rather than its cause), it will be apparent that there are many common factors. Plans dealing with consequences will hold across a broad spectrum of potential risks, with three main exceptions:

- The nature of each type of threat does need to be considered, in case there are specific considerations that need to be taken into account.

- The plan should always cater for the worst case scenario.

- The plan does need to be flexible. There are no rules governing the way in which a crisis will actually take place, or the level of its impact.

A business continuity plan can begin to take shape through visualizing the effects of a disaster unfolding. There are three stages to this visualization:

- the incident stage;

- the recovery stage; and

- the continuity stage.

At every stage, an organization must ask how potential damage can be mitigated, making a distinction between what can be done in advance (precautionary measures) and what can be done subsequently (response measures).

Managing an incident

Physical steps can and should be taken. Many may consist of enhancements of existing health and safety schemes. For instance, office buildings should be designed or adapted to reduce the risk of injury from an explosion – improved glazing, designated bomb shelter areas and efficient, robust internal communications systems, with back-up.

A key issue at this stage is moving staff and members of the public to a place of safety. To continue the terrorism example, where a vehicle bomb threat exists, external evacuation of a business premises will depend on staff and visitors to the premises getting themselves outside as the police cordon off the surrounding area as quickly as possible. Alternative staff assembly areas must be envisaged, as it is impossible to predict in advance where the cordon will stretch to and which areas will consequently be off-limits. In the aftermath of a major incident of this sort, staff will need to be able to contact one another for reassurance, mutual support and guidance. It is therefore an important consideration to ensure that an effective telephone contact system is in place to enable an affected business to begin the first stage of recovery.

Working methods should be in place to ensure that each member of staff's whereabouts can be accounted for throughout the working day. This can be achieved through an attendance register, or through line managers taking responsibility for their respective team's presence and whereabouts.

A useful structure for this stage can be summarized by the following:

- spreading the alert;
- establishing control;
- moving staff and members of the public to a place of safety; and
- reporting to headquarters, where appropriate.

The recovery stage

The aim of a recovery plan is to anticipate how extra resources can be brought in on the point of crisis. The minimum requirements (including a time-scale) needed for the business to stay in operation should be assessed. There should be a focus on issues such as expected level of output, speed of delivery and quality standards, and an assessment of the resources needed to achieve these targets, across all key areas, such as premises, staff, finance, supplies, facilities' records, logistics and communications.

An action plan must be in place, rehearsed and proven effective to deal with the consequences of a crisis. At least one individual in each business location should be responsible for designing and maintaining the action plan. It is important that the plan has clearly designated objectives that apply to the particular circumstances of the business and its location.

In large businesses, it may be helpful to have a division of labour in which there is a *co-ordinating group* and a *recovery team*. The co-ordinating group should be able to activate a rapid-response list of essential staff to constitute a recovery team. The list must be updated regularly and contain data from up-to-date contact records. The recovery team needs to draw on a cross-section of disciplines, encompassing all the important business fields – facilities, IT, personnel, communications and so on. Salvage experts should also be on the team. The recovery team requires sufficient autonomy to take decisions and initiate courses of action without constantly having to refer to the co-ordinating group. In short, the system must be streamlined and flexible. Recovery team members must be able to think for themselves.

The recovery stage begins as soon as the consequences of an incident become clear. The plan should account for a range of worst-case assumptions, including the following:

- The business premises have to be evacuated for at least one working day, possibly longer.

- The premises are severely damaged and it may be impossible for staff to return to them for a significant period of time.

- Assuming either of the above are the case, business recovery prospects will be significantly affected, specifically:
  - staff will quite possibly be amongst the casualties;
  - work in progress will be disrupted;
  - the business will immediately lose access to materials, equipment, records, stock and so on;
  - unsecured items will have been exposed to the blast, and quite possibly to subsequent looting and/or consequent damage;
  - communications facilities will be disabled;
  - lost power could corrupt or terminally damage computer data;
  - material stored offsite may be out of date, depending on how frequently it has been kept backed-up; and
  - the incident will inevitably be widely reported and, as a consequence, there may be a directly linked decline in consumer confidence.

Precautionary measures should be put in place to minimize the severity of the above factors taking place. These may include:

- Proper building design to take account of the effects of an explosion or similar threat.

- A 'clear desk' policy - that is to say, when papers are not actually in use, they are stored in secure cupboards and/or cabinets, meaning that important and/or confidential documents are less likely to be scattered after the event.

- Office equipment should be covered when not in use to minimize collateral damage.

- An efficient data back-up system should be in place and data should be stored at least 1 km away (in the case of a bomb, outside any police cordon). This also applies to any important paperwork, including insurance policies and any current contracts with disaster recovery specialists and/or salvage firms.

● Information on key staff members (identities and contact numbers) should also be kept away from the premises, where it can be readily retrieved by the security co-ordinator. By the same token, staff should have been thoroughly rehearsed in what to do in the event of a disaster of this magnitude having taken place – this would include issuing alternative contact numbers to family and friends, to avoid jamming the main switchboard numbers.

● Management should ensure that the designated staff members are aware of the need to review all appropriate insurance policies on a regular basis, and to make sure that they do indeed cover all the potential losses that the business might suffer. Remember that terrorist cover may have to be bought separately. Asset registers need to be very carefully maintained, as well as being kept off site with other important documentation and data.

IT disaster recovery

Computer systems are becoming vital for most companies to operate properly. However, it is only fairly recently that companies started to think about what might happen if their mainframe or server suddenly breaks down, or is ruined by a natural disaster such as a fire.

Many companies are now undertaking contingency planning, or disaster recovery planning. In the area of finance, disaster recovery planning is becoming mandatory, because of new regulations introduced by the Bank of England and the Financial Services Authority. Regulators in other industries such as telecommunications, the utilities sectors and the health service are now considering the same.

Priority tasks for the co-ordinating group and recovery team

Using again the example of the aftermath of a terrorist bomb attack, the following are key tasks for the specially designated teams to undertake (with direct reference to the Home Office publication '*Maximising business resilience to terrorist bombings*'):

- A crisis management centre needs to be set up, with all essential services. The action plan needs to identify this centre and how it will be equipped.

- Emergency services must be contacted.

- Immediate welfare needs of staff members must be met.

- All staff must be accounted for.

- Staff must be transported home in safety.

- Families need to be contacted and reassured.

- Hospital visits need to be planned and follow-up care considered.

- Staff need to be properly reassured and, where appropriate, reimbursed.

- Care and counselling should be provided.

- All developments should be regularly reported to head office through secure communications channels.

- Immediate action should be taken to preserve vital resources.

- Media contacts should be established and a spokesman appointed.

- All assistance necessary should be given to rescue and security services as appropriate.

Where the impact of a crisis has not been as severe as, for example, a terrorist bomb, the action plan may follow a different, less radical, course.

As the Home Office plan states, there are essentially four priorities in the re-establishment phase – people, premises, product and purchasers – examined in more detail below:

- **People:** The workforce of an organization needs to be highly motivated if it is to emerge from a crisis with as little damage as possible. This makes staff care an immediate and continuing priority. A business that overlooks the human factor when attempting to limit financial damage will inevitably suffer staff retention problems in future. All staff should be phoned as soon as possible after the event to ensure that their welfare is properly addressed. As time elapses post-crisis, staff will need to move from stand-by to some form of mobilization. They will inevitably require clear instructions. Transport may be needed. Rotas may be required and refreshments must be available. Staff need to be paid on time, irrespective of the scale and extent of the crisis and the subsequent disruption. It may be important to pay overtime and this should be budgeted for.

- **Premises:** For larger organizations operating in more than one building, it may well be possible to relocate all displaced personnel to an alternative office location. It may be advisable to consider contracting in advance with one of the specialist business continuity firms which guarantee to provide alternative premises at short notice. When attempting to plan for this type of eventuality, it is important to take into account the range and depth of back-up services required. This applies to IT, telecommunications equipment and other specialist equipment. Telephone requirements are vitally important – it is important to remember that in the aftermath of a crisis, organizations tend to be besieged by phone enquiries. Additional staff may well need to be drafted in to cope with the upsurge in demand. It may be helpful to consider diverting calls to head office during this time.

- **Product:** The bottom line is that organizations need to get back into full production post-crisis. Key priorities include: recovering important records; recovering details of work in hand; setting up accounting systems and cost centres; preparing the insurance claim; and liaising with other branches to ensure that as much support as possible is ready and waiting.

- **Purchasers:** All customers and suppliers will be following reports of the crisis closely. There may be justifiable doubts concerning the ability of a business to continue trading. As a result, stakeholders may seek reassurance in the aftermath. Others will simply shift allegiance to competitors rather than risk any disruption in supply/service. Contacting customers is therefore an urgent priority as soon as possible after the crisis – customers can be prioritized in order of business importance. Larger companies may want to designate specific teams to phone/fax important clients (it is therefore crucial to ensure that an up-to-date database of customers is kept off site). They may also want to set up a helpdesk. It can be helpful to initiate limited and targeted advertising campaigns, as well as – naturally – providing helpful, positive interviews to the media. Where negative reports have been released, these should be countered as a matter of urgency.

Staff members should not be permitted to give interviews without authorization from the co-ordinating group, and where pre-appointed individuals do give interviews, these should follow a pre-agreed line. It can be highly damaging for conflicting interviews to be given out. Trade and representative organizations can be used to disseminate messages. Experience shows that it is far better to give out regular bulletins stating that matters are being dealt with as fast as possible, rather than attempting to maintain a low profile.

Getting back to normal

The only thing that a business can rely upon post-crisis is that circumstances will have changed. It is impossible to predict exactly how. A degree of flexibility is crucial so that management can adapt existing strategies to cope with a new environment.

The business continuity plan can help to sketch out this process, however. The business premises will need to be 're-colonized' and returned to full working order – this means that plans of pre-existing systems and office organization need to be kept off site and referred to in the aftermath. Properly planned contracts with salvage firms will speed up the redistribution and removal of key assets. Contractors should be identified in the planning stage to ensure their quality – instead of coping with an onslaught of sales pitches post-crisis. Lease requirements on office premises should be checked to enable prompt identification of rent rebates/requirements in the event that the premises prove to be uninhabitable for a limited period of time.

Handling the media

An external public-relations consultancy firm may be the preferred choice for handling the media and negotiating a clear path through the vagaries of post-crisis fall-out. Contact with journalists is inevitable in the aftermath of any such event, and this contact should be something which management feels comfortable with. Media training is an important part of the crisis management armoury – it will be important for company spokespeople to stand in front of the camera and give out a rehearsed and consistent message. And it should be the leadership of an organization that speaks out – commitment to stakeholders is under intense pressure in the post-crisis period and senior management are the ones who must make every effort (visible and behind the scenes) to ensure that confidence is restored as swiftly as possible.

Post-crisis – the longer term

Preparation for the short-term effects of a crisis taking place is one thing: a frequent area where organizations overlook potential damage and disruption is the longer-term fall-out, however. Many organizations have a tendency within them – and especially so in particular countries – to function as blame cultures. This is clearly counter-productive – once a crisis has taken place, been assimilated into onward activity and its effects controlled, there is no point in pursuing blame-based analysis beyond any areas of direct responsibility. For example, in Japan, organizations increase their exposure to crisis damage because of the real reluctance employees have to break bad news. An organization's culture must ensure that it manages crisis risk and learns from the process. In short, crisis management is less science and more culture.

Thinking about the bigger picture

It is not enough to devote time and resources to putting a plan in place. For a start, the plan needs to be tested and rehearsed on a regular basis. It needs to be upgraded, to take account of any change in working environments. The organization as a whole needs to know that a plan exists and requires some knowledge of it. Insurance cover is also a factor. Is the organizational insurance programme the most appropriate, bearing in mind business risk types? (See Chapter 2 for a fuller discussion of insurance options.) It is also critical that an organization can respond to a disaster out of hours: disasters, of their nature, do not abide by regular patterns and timetables. Another dimension to crisis management that needs to be considered is the prospect that suppliers might have crises themselves.

Crisis management – key points at a glance

A crisis may vary, according to:

- Size and scale – a few computers down or a whole network?

- Visibility – is it happening behind the scenes?

- Complexity level – are there sufficient resources and people with specialist skills to deal with the crisis?

Depending on the nature of an organization and its business activities, a crisis may arise as the result of a wide range of incidents, including:

- criminal activities, including terrorism;

- kidnap;

- extortion;

- accident, including fire/explosion;

- product failure/contamination, perhaps leading to injury and product recall;

- health and safety disasters;

- negative public/media opinion, perhaps resulting from management actions;

- employee dissent, perhaps leading to sabotage;

- physical disaster; or

- unexpected death of a key executive.

The aim of a crisis management plan is to:

- reduce to the minimum all possible risks to health and safety;

- enable the organization to make a fast, co-ordinated, thoroughly rehearsed response to any crisis, the magnitude or cause of which will not be known until it occurs; and

- minimize the long-term damage to the business.

Crisis managers aim to:

- prevent a crisis happening;

- plan response and recovery programmes, allocate responsibilities among personnel and train staff in procedures and roles;

- deal with a crisis once it occurs;

- deal with the effects of crisis and aspects of communication; and

- oversee response and recovery programmes.

The development of a crisis management plan should take into account all aspects of internal and external communications arising from a crisis. A crisis management plan should address:

- those 'worst case' scenarios that have been identified (e.g. product contamination, extortion, major systems failure);

- collation and analysis of facts as they become known in the course of a crisis;

- organization (roles and responsibilities) of those individuals to be involved in the management of a crisis;

- internal communication guidelines covering as a minimum:
  - media;
  - authorities;
  - public;
  - customers;
  - shareholder; and
  - competitors.

A crisis management plan should be:

- Simple to use – in a crisis the plan should be accessible, easy-to-read, a fast source of help. Manuals should not run into hundreds of pages.

- Clearly indexed – sections should be indexed by corporate policy, organization and by specific crises.

The crisis management plan should contain:

- Corporate policy – the protection of people and the environment should supersede any other priority, including commercial interests, to ensure speed of communications, clarity of instructions and essential confidentiality. The most senior tier should be primarily concerned with monitoring the incident and authorizing decisions at a strategic level. The two-tiered organization may be comprised of:
  - a co-ordinating group; and
  - a recovery team.

A brief description of the roles and responsibilities of each of these is set out below.

The co-ordinating group (CG)

The function of this body is to develop strategy and make major decisions. It has no real implementation role. It may comprise of not more than four or five executives, with others 'on call' who may join the group as and when required. Core team members may include:

- CEO;

- CFO;

- COO;

- production/technical specialists;

- public relations;

- legal; and

- co-ordinator.

Other team members should remain on call until they are

needed or the crisis is resolved:

- human resource management;
- safety;
- environment;
- security;
- international;
- medical;
- sales and marketing;
- logistics;
- government relations; and
- finance.

The co-ordinator has an extremely important role to play in ensuring continuity and is the link between the CG and recovery team that implements the CG's decisions. The co-ordinator is likely to be an executive who commands respect and has the authority to make decisions and authorize expenditure. All global site communications should be channelled to the CG through the co-ordinator who will decide whether the incident is sufficiently serious to merit a meeting of the CG. In many organizations, the co-ordinator may dedicate as much as 10 per cent of their time to ensuring that policies and procedures are up-to-date and tested.

The issues that the CG might have to address include:

- crisis management organization;
- responsibility for decision making;
- delegation to lower levels of management, or to outside authorities;
- degree of consultation with other agencies including emer-

gency services, police, government authorities, families, other organizations, joint venture partners, etc.;

- compliance with legal and regulatory requirements;

- acceptance of risk – to the victims, to the public, to the organization and its shareholders in terms of liability and financial loss;

- media policy;

- internal communications; and

- direction and supervision of the recovery team.

The scale of management resources required to support the CG during an environmental incident, for example, may make it necessary to form specialist support groups. For example:

- Public relations team – may be tasked with managing:
  - organization of media facilities;
  - drafting and issuing responses;
  - spokespeople; and
  - dealing with media, public enquiries and environmental groups.

- Human resource management – tasked with supporting victims and managing communications with families/next-of-kin.

- Technical/safety – research and advise on related problems.

- External affairs – contacts with outside agencies such as environmental and health agencies, local councils, and governments.

The recovery team (RT)

The function of the on-site RT is to take all executive action to resolve the incident within the policy parameters set by the CG and under their direction. This team should represent those parts of the organization involved in the crisis. Depending on circumstances the team members may include:

- plant director;
- operations manager;
- technical specialists;
- safety representative;
- quality assurance manager;
- logistics;
- sales;
- local PR representative;
- human resource management; and
- finance.

The responsibilities of the RT may include:

- local incident management;
- local liaison with emergency services;
- local liaison with environmental and health agencies;
- local liaison with policy;
- local liaison with other government authorities;
- local liaison with other affected companies;
- victim support – also family support and briefing if appropriate;
- local media handling;
- local liaison with environmental groups;
- information to CG on local situation; and
- advice to CG on local risks.

Alerting – procedures and communications

Detailed instructions are prepared and issued at all levels within the crisis management organization in order to ensure that incidents are reported rapidly and that the respective management levels are alerted. This system must be capable of functioning on a $24 \times 7 \times 365$ basis, including absences of key members of management.

The alerting system and the two levels of crisis management must be supported by efficient and secure communication systems on a $24 \times 7 \times 365$ basis.

Training and testing

To ensure that the crisis management procedures work and are well understood, all personnel likely to be involved in an incident should receive crisis management training. This training should cover organization and procedures. Also, spokespeople at CG and RT levels should be given media training to reflect high-pressure, realistic crisis situations. All procedures must be tested fully and amended to reflect 'lessons learned'.

Operational risk issues for the twenty-first century

Introduction

The successful management of operational change in the new millennium is set to become even more critical to overall business success as the rate of change continues to increase. Organizations will need to adapt even more quickly to the changing needs of their marketplace. They will be able to pick and choose from an expanding array of technological solutions to reorganize business processes and further restructure. In operating in 'network economies', they will be able to enter into new forms of risk-sharing business-to-business relationships. In all of these contexts, the tension between managing risk and taking risk will be even higher.

The management of growth and change, in tandem with operations management, will be a key concern. In the 1980s and 1990s, cost-cutting exercises, rationalization initiatives, and other attempts to create 'mean and lean' enterprises took centre stage. In the new millennium, a return to investment-led growth is likely to highlight the importance of managing growth, change, and operational continuity in new ways.

As the pace of change increases exponentially, the role of operational risk management will gravitate even further towards ensuring that business operations are as efficient as possible in delivering service to the customer. Risk management practice will have to make the transition towards satisfying all stakeholders, such as customers and employees in addition to shareholders.

In this chapter, we examine new business trends that require a cutting edge application of operational risk management. Integration is emerging as a key concept. As we move into the millennium, the challenge for strategic decision-makers is to forge links between risk management and strategy, value, capital management, finance, corporate culture, operations, and customer service. Organizations that can achieve this will really start to manage risk for competitive advantage. Only then can risk management be equated with managing change for the organization as a whole.

The banking sector is more advanced than any other in working towards these objectives. Following regulatory pressure, banks are now taking a strategic approach to ensuring operational continuity. By minimizing risk on their operations side, banks can maximize risk with their use of capital for strategic advantage and increased shareholder value. Lessons are there to be learned for organizations in other industry sectors, as they strive to define, assess and manage operational risk in the most efficient way possible.

Elsewhere, e-business is a classic example of the need for an integrated approach to risk and reward. The Internet demonstrates, for example, that managing supply of service and customer demand is even more difficult than in conventional markets. The need for operational resilience is absolutely central, coupled with an appropriate degree of risk taking. So far, companies have been keen to take advantage of e-business opportunities, but, in jumping in too quickly, have lost sight of operational risk management issues that have a key bearing on the success or failure of a new venture.

The section on risk and restructuring examines how organizations can maximize the risk:return ratio by establishing shared service centres and entering into joint ventures and mergers.

Finally, we examine some responses to new corporate requirements, such as those embodied in the Turnbull report.

The chapter as a whole is structured as follows:

1 Financial institutions at the leading edge;

2 Changes in the e-business world;

3 Risk and restructuring:

- shared service centres

- joint ventures

- mergers and acquisitions

4 Corporate governance pressures.

Financial institutions at the leading edge

Introduction

The sophistication of operational risk management practices and their implementation is not uniform across sectors. For those lagging behind, there may be significant lessons to be learned from the leaders. Evidence so far suggests that cutting-edge applications of operational risk management are fast emerging in the banking sector. This is not surprising. Financial institutions are very heavily reliant on technology and are heavily exposed to the risks associated with highly complex operations and, in particular, vast quantities of data flowing through hundreds of systems – most of which are critical to operational success.

Institutions face a huge range of risks, including fraud, systems failure, illegal trading, theft, natural disaster, and errors in processing data. The potential for errors that cause loss is huge, and can only be mitigated if appropriate checks and balances are in place. The risk of more immediate monetary loss is higher in banks because capital management, in one form or another, is at the core of their operations. As a result, enhanced management, controls and monitoring in reducing such incidents, play a vital role.

Banking is by its very nature a high-risk business. Bank managers, regulators, policy makers and investors have a natural desire to want assurances that risk controls are in place. The need for operational risk management has become more apparent in the last few years because of major, high-profile losses suffered by Barings, Daiwa, NatWest and Sumitomo, among others.

Operational risk exposure is intimately linked to systemic risk – the risk that one bank failure could lead to others. The integration of financial markets now tends to mean that a failure in one part will affect the whole system. All banks are linked to global payments systems that could bring the banking sector to a halt if part of them failed.

However, the case for operational risk management is not just made by banking failure. For the individual bank, the consequences of not managing operational risk on an on-going basis are constantly evident. A significant level of actual losses, costs and write-offs are reported internally each year. Again, these risks are not solely financial. One bank recently discovered that in one year alone significant financial losses caused by regulatory action and censure, loss of income, legal action, adverse publicity and loss of business were the direct consequences of operational risk incidents.

The rationale for managing operational risk is not merely defensive. Banks have a direct financial interest to grapple with and understand operational risk. The main reason is that more accurate capital measurement leads to more efficient deployment of that capital. Banks do not want to put aside more capital to cater for the possibility of financial loss than they need to. After accounting for market and credit risk, measurement of operational risk offers the potential for discovering an excess, which could be invested more profitably back in operations.

Definitions

At least since the 1970s, bankers have measured and hedged market risk – the volatility risk they face from market variables, such as currency rates, behaving unexpectedly. In the 1980s, it was realized that, in the face of countries like Mexico defaulting on debt repayments, banks would have to pay more attention to credit risk. Some banks have pioneered risk management systems. Two leaders are the US banks JP Morgan and Bankers Trust. JP Morgan has developed a credit risk measurement system called CreditMetrics, among others, and Bankers Trust has pioneered a variety of capital-at-risk measures including RAROC (risk adjusted return on capital).

Today, there is a now a discussion underway on how to allocate capital to cover operational risks. This is set to become a critical competitive and regulatory issue. Regulators and central banks – under criticism for their role and responsibilities for various banking failures in the last few years – have been keen to restructure their supervisory systems and ensure that effective self-regulation takes place.

Unlike market and credit risk that have developed clear-cut meanings, there is as yet no universally agreed definition of operational risk. Some banks define it as the risk arising from various types of human and technical error. Most banks associate operational risk with all business lines, including infrastructure.

All banks see a relationship between market, credit and operational risk exposure and realize the importance of managing those exposures in an integrated manner. More banks are questioning the point of having expensive, state-of-the-art market risk management systems if one rogue trader can bankrupt the institution in a matter of weeks. On other levels there are many correlations between the different types of risk. An operational problem – say with a settlement failure – could create credit or market risk, for instance. At its simplest, rogue traders convert the risk inherent in markets into direct operational risks. As one CEO commented following a recent derivatives loss:

> 'These instruments always carry a trading risk. What we did not allow for in them was the operational risk involved in supervising the people trading in them.'

ORM has been called 'the last piece in the puzzle' for banks wishing actively to protect themselves against the unexpected but at the same time, optimize their risk-taking behaviour. As such it follows the concerted effort to manage market and credit risk. Operational risk management was recently defined by the Basle Committee on Banking Supervision, a committee of banking supervisory authorities established by the Central Bank of the Group Ten Countries in 1975, as:

> 'Breakdowns in internal controls and corporate governance ... [which] can lead to financial losses, through error, fraud, or failure to perform in a timely manner or cause the interests of the bank to be compromised ... by its dealers, lending officers or other staff exceeding their authority, or conducting their business in an unethical or risky manner.'

Operational risk has also been defined as:

> 'Major failure of information technology systems or events such as major fires or other disasters.'

Until fairly recently, ORM has been the only risk component that does not have a senior person devoted to setting policy, in contrast to market and credit risk. Responsibility for operational risk exposures has been decentralized across human resources managers, technology managers, general operations staff and premises management. Banks are only now starting to institutionalize operational risk management committees. Those that do so are finding that they can increase the efficiency of their resources. For example, a significant amount of effort is often put into risk management in banks, but in an uncoordinated and 'silo' fashion. Whenever risk incidents occur, days are spent investigating, analysing, reporting and responding. Coordinated policies can ensure that effort is not wasted and targeted effectively, maximizing the value of the people involved.

Increased operational risk

Banks face the same operational risks as other organizations, such as fire and explosion, business interruption, technology, brand impairment, directors' liability and so on. However, the financial sector has experienced enhanced risk exposure due to the following four key factors:

- the globalization of markets;

- loosening of credit policies;

- systems proliferation; and

- rapid and strategic change.

Risk is often increased when these developments interact with changed circumstances within banks themselves, such as:

- new business/products – which may be processed outside existing core systems: risks may be high until procedures have been imbedded in;

- human resources: loss of key staff will have an impact, as will inadequate experience and insufficient resource; and

- information technology: loss of key systems, inadequate maintenance, or new development and inappropriate software.

Operational risk tends to be more critical in business lines with high volume, high turnover (transactions/time), high degree of structural change, and/or complex support systems. Operational risk has a high potential impact in these areas. Crucially, the risk is magnified if the businesses also have low margins.

Globalization of markets

The advance of telecommunications has meant that transactions can be originated anywhere in the world in a matter of seconds. Money can be moved around the world in a much shorter space of time than previously.

For banks, the ability to predict market movements and protect against what they cannot predict has become essential. Losses of $100m can now take place in seconds, wiping out a month of profits. Risk exposure has increased because counterparties can transact with the bank in multiple locations at the same time, increasing or decreasing the bank's exposure by large amounts.

Globalization in the sense of the spread of banking activities around the world also points to the futility of regulations designed to cope with national, and therefore separate, markets.

Easing of credit policies

In the recession of the early 1990s, many banks wrote off many of their loans and adopted more conservative credit policies. As a result, many believed that a period of caution had embraced the sector. Increased competition for lending, however, has led to a greater willingness on the part of banks to take risks again.

Systems proliferation

Operating risk has increased with the use of new technology. Inputs into systems may not be detected and may result in actual cash transfers resulting in losses. In the worse-case scenario, systems may fail.

Rapid and strategic change

As competition in many markets has increased, banks are finding that they need to adopt rapid strategic and structural change on a constant basis.

Some of these changes may include:

- increased transaction volumes;

- reengineering of business processes and technology; and

- new products and new business relationships (i.e. joint ventures).

The role of regulation in banking risk management

The development of capital adequacy standards – the putting aside of capital as a cushion against potential loss – has taken place in three distinct phases: pre-Basle; regulatory capital; and a strategic focus which goes beyond regulatory constraints towards a notion of economic risk capital.

Pre-Basle, regulatory requirements were basic. There was little focus on capital adequacy. Balance-sheet management tended to be driven by liquidity and asset regulatory requirements. Capital was mainly considered for structural funding and long-term capital expenditure.

The 1988 Basle minimal capital rules for banks have been widely adopted around the world as a basic criterion for measuring bank stability. They helped to shift the emphasis from building assets for their own sake towards strengthening the capital base. Banks realized the need to be well-capitalized, in order to gain the trust of observers, ratings agencies, analysts, customers and their own peers. As the derivatives markets grew, for instance, awareness grew of the need for a buffer for the increased risks. For banks, this was not a defensive measure: it has immediate benefits for profitability.

In 1997, the Basle Committee introduced its 'preconditions for effective banking supervision'. According to the Basle Committee, 'the principles represent the basic elements of an effective supervisory system. They are comprehensive in their coverage, addressing the preconditions for effective banking supervision, licensing and structure, prudential regulations and requirements, methods of ongoing banking supervision, formal powers of supervisors and cross-border banking'.

Tools for assessing operational risk in financial services

As operational risk management gains increasing credibility in the financial services, banks are using a range of tools to analyse people, processes and technologies to identify where operational risks lie. More sophisticated banks are relaying that data on an increasingly regular basis to senior management so it can be acted on at the strategic level. The logical conclusion of this process is the use of economic capital modelling for operational risk. As yet, however, few banks have reached this stage. Different organizations are at different 'stages of maturity' in their ability to assess operational risk with a high degree of accuracy. These may be considered as:

- **Stage 1: Assess.** Senior management acknowledges that their organization needs to be more proactive and deliberate in understanding operational risk. The first steps include identifying risk, defining controls, ensuring that the business units are willing to take responsibility for risks and creating tools (considered below) so that the data can be collected, as well as constructing a database to aid this process. Tools applicable for this stage include self-assessment and risk process maps.

- **Stage 2: Track.** This comprises an interpretation of the impact of the risks that have been identified. Management is now in a better position to quantify the impact, with the help of tools such as risk indicators/trackers and escalation triggers.

- **Stage 3: Quantify.** Here, the tools mentioned above are used to change the course of the business, through proactive risk avoidance. The tool most appropriate for this stage is a data analytical tool that can be used to conduct analysis on the causes and management of certain risks. The overall aim is for risk quantification to be used as decision support for senior management.

The end objective of operational risk assessment is to understand the cost of operational risk management. As well as incorporating financial loss, this 'cost' should include the cost of lost customers and damaged reputation, as well as the cost of resources and time in mitigating and managing risk. An estimate of this cost is a crucial pre-requisite for any capital allocation process to occur.

The most useful tools here are the loss event database and the use of risk-based modelling. A risk-based model, which is a statistical and actuarial model, can use the data of actual operational risk events, build distributions of the severity in the event that a loss occurs, and conduct a Monte Carlo analysis between frequency and severity to build a distribution of events. Using a given level of confidence, a value-at-risk analysis can be calculated for each operational risk and for each business line. These models can be calibrated for each institution and can incorporate hedging or insurance programmes.

Operational risk assessment, therefore, is the first stage in enabling risk management and performance measurement to be closely related. For example, if this is to be successful, the risk assessment approach should capture significant, high severity events as well as smaller incidents which have a more continuous financial effect, not to mention, when aggregated, an effect on customer service delivery, reputation and, ultimately, shareholder value.

The effectiveness of operational risk assessment partly depends on establishing the right management framework, however. New risk assessment projects need to have won internal buy-in and should be directed from senior management level. At the same time, individual business units need to be responsible and accountable for quantifying the risks, since, internally, they are the closest to them and are likely to have the greatest understanding of them. This relationship between senior management and individual business units is key if risk assessment is to be effective. For instance, it is only through the collection and presentation of the right data that senior management action to mitigate risk can be effective.

Risk assessment tools

Self-assessment

Self-assessments tools are a series of questionnaires or workshops to gain greater understanding of the operational risks facing an organization. They may vary in their sophistication and thoroughness, ranging from perhaps twenty questions to thousands that cut across processes and organizational functions. Most organizations start self-assessment by listing the controls and compliance they require from different business units. In more advanced cases, questionnaires may ask for more detailed information on the extent to which controls are in place and how risks are being monitored. Alongside these questionnaires, workshops may be used to gather more comprehensive data.

Ideally, the operational mechanics should be in place for risk assessments to be run quarterly. The key challenge is management buy-in. The information generated should be consistent with the information that management needs to run their business. For a start, management has to reject the idea that operational risk management is an unnecessary overhead that they could do without.

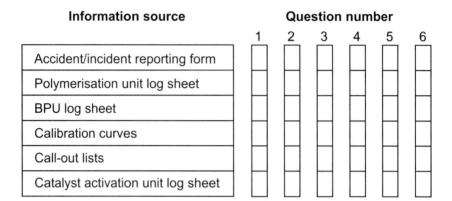

Information source   **Question number**

	1	2	3	4	5	6
Accident/incident reporting form						
Polymerisation unit log sheet						
BPU log sheet						
Calibration curves						
Call-out lists						
Catalyst activation unit log sheet						

Q1   How important is the information source to you personally in your job?
Q2   How often do you usually refer to this source?
Q3   Is the information usually accurate?
Q4   How quickly can you find the information you want?
Q5   How often does the information normally get changed?
Q6   Would it help if, in addition to having information on paper as now, you
     or your team could also quickly access the information on a computer
     screen in the control room?

Figure 4.1 Sample self-assessment questionnaire

Risk maps/process flows

A risk map is an overview of an organization's processes, business units and functions, outlining where key risks lie. As they
are intended as a comprehensive bottom-up tool, they are an
effective way to allocate responsibility and accountability for
risks down to the level of individual line managers. In addition, they are useful for defining weak points in the chain of
where risk should be managed. However, a potential drawback is that, like self-assessments, the data collected is mainly
qualitative and may not be in a form conducive to decision
support for senior managers.

Risk indicators

Unlike the previous two tools, risk indicators supply quantitative data to managers in standalone reports that detail the extent to which organizations are exposed to particular risks. They are more helpful in aiding decision making at the senior management level. Typical risks may include the number of failed trades in a given time period, the number and severity of errors, and so on. According to which risks are being tracked, risk indicators can provide information to managers on a daily, monthly, and yearly basis. Managers can use the information as an indicator that certain risks need to be managed more proactively, and to facilitate day-to-day decision making more generally. Risk indicators are also useful for their correlation effect; certain patterns of correlations between risks can emerge, leading managers to establish key linkages, such as that, hypothetically, between the proportion of temporary staff and particular errors.

Risk indicators give managers predictive information so that they can act on issues before they become major problems to the organization. One of their weaknesses, however, is that the link between the risk indicator and actual loss resulting from it may be unproven or speculative. Risk indicators alone will not inform managers of the business consequences of the risks faced. Escalation triggers, considered next, can help to overcome this limitation as they are set in the knowledge of past, actual incidents.

Escalation triggers

Escalation triggers are used in conjunction with risk indicators and are critical limits or warning signals that should trigger some form of predetermined action on the part of management. They tend to be set in the knowledge of the lead-up to a more major operational risk event. They are also defined in relation to the level of risk-taking that an organization finds acceptable. For example, an organization with a high risk tolerance may set their escalation triggers high before any action kicks in, in the hope that they are maximizing opportunity and profit. Overall, escalation triggers act as a further method of giving managers decision support.

Loss event database

A loss event database is able to capture and accumulate individual loss events across businesses and risk types. Data collection is a particular issue, since without a comprehensive use of the formal tools, data often remains fragmented throughout the organization. Data on low-frequency, high-severity risks is also hard to come by. Other operational risks, by their nature, are hard to put into figures, especially certain HR and people related risks.

There are three main applications:

- **empirical analysis:** when qualitative data can be analysed in order to assess the effectiveness of current risk policies and controls;

- **quantifying the loss from past operational events:** this can help to place a value on operational risk management; and

- **modelling of potential operational risk events in the future:** data can be used in a predictive fashion, perhaps for the purpose of allocating capital to cover those risk exposures or to aid a decision-making process.

Some examples of risk indicators may include:

- human resources: the level of temporary help, staff turnover, training budget, vacation and absence;

- business: audit score, customer satisfaction rating, customer complaints;

- IT: system downtime, number of system problems; and

- operations: settlement, accounting losses, number of losses, evaluation losses.

Improving operational risk assessment

To a large extent, the effectiveness of these tools depends on an integrated approach. The effectiveness of each tool is dependent on the success of the tool that preceded it, until an effective database is built. To date, however, the evolution of risk assessment tools has tended to occur on a fragmented basis. One of the challenges is to move towards a more quantitative approach with the use of more quantitative tools. Another is the use of more leading indicators that have a predictive value. Some critical areas for fresh analysis may include:

- rising volumes, and the active monitoring of activity versus capacity;

- unresolved problems, which include open issues such as increasing activity of all types, staff shortness and the numbers of customer complaints;

- productivity, which could be linked back to the numbers of experienced versus temporary staff;

- employee morale, such as the numbers of employees leaving the company; and

- causal analysis, which includes tracking and correlating errors and losses to their underlying drivers, such as products and sales teams, among other factors.

Information gathering is, in many ways, the foundation upon which more effective risk assessment is based. One improvement that could be made is in estimating the indirect, as well as financial, costs of operational risk events. Another is the increased use of sharing event data across institutions to foster understanding of low frequency high severity events.

Finally, while operational risk management is often seen as a back office issue, increasing attention will need to be paid to front office activity where often complex instruments can lead to increased risk. Improving training is a key area to make this happen.

In summary, for success in operational risk assessment, there needs to be the raw data to work on, a theory or framework to make sense of that data, and finally, the commitment from senior management to sanction the resources and make use of the data for decision support. The three key pillars are, therefore:

- data availability;

- measurement techniques; and

- management acceptance.

The future of ORM in banking

Sound operational risk management will be a core competency of financial services companies

The business model for corporations globally is changing. Firms are now executing according to their own core competencies and beginning to outsource what other firms can do better and cheaper. As firms examine the value chain of service, from origination through servicing and accounting, they are re-examining where they add value to servicing customers. Areas that do not add value are subject to restructuring. Operational risk management becomes a core competency to help organizations excel in any component of the value chain and to manage external partner relationships.

Shareholders and the investment community will also demand evidence of good practice and punish banks' mistakes. Proactive risk management will directly reduce cost and the volatility of earnings. One bank recently announced a surprise to earnings due to an operational event and the stock price dropped over 20 per cent in a single day. The price of failure can be very high and will continue to get higher in the future.

Competition adds to the pressure to improve operational risk management. Sound risk management will become synonymous with good customer service – accurate data, timely response, few errors or disputes, solid ethics, and the comfort of dealing with a firm with a good reputation. The consequences of not having a good operational risk management programme can be extreme – from falling volume to ultimate failure or being forced to accept a merger or acquisition.

Regulators are looking for a comprehensive risk management framework and capital allocation methodologies that recognize operational risk and create the right internal behavioural incentives.

Financial service firms will be increasingly dependent on taking operational risk

Many top financial firms are moving away from risk-taking to more focused businesses and fee-based services. High earnings-based volatility has reduced risk-taking strategies. Market making and distribution strategies with lower risk profiles are becoming more central. There is also an increased focus on fee-based businesses that provide stable low-risk income, with high return on equity.

These fee-based businesses (custody, trust, asset management and brokerage business) take little market or credit risk but do take significant operational risks. With the industry shifting to rely more and more on fee-based services, the levels of operational risk will grow proportionally.

An additional factor is that financial markets are becoming more and more commoditized. A new product today is a standard product tomorrow. This means higher volumes and lower margins across the industry. Firms will not be able to afford a major operational loss since there is less room for error. Those firms with top-notch programmes, generating close to zero defects in processing, will be the new superior performers.

All across industry, reengineering efforts are reducing costs. Streamlined operations and automation may reduce operational risks or potentially increase them. The outcome depends on the effectiveness of an operational framework and implementation plan. For example, straight-through processing and redesigned business models leave fewer people involved. This change can reduce operational risk because there is less manual intervention and exceptions are highlighted. However, the staff that have traditionally dealt with exceptions, middle management, are being eliminated. These staff are often the most knowledgeable and most active in managing operational risk on a day-to-day basis. Without a proper operational risk management framework, procedures, training, and ongoing communications in the implementation phase, cost reduction initiatives can increase operational risk.

A need that arises from this trend will be product/transaction approval processes to ensure risks are well controlled before firms start to do business. Firms will have to rely on automation to perform some controls and get the transactions booked and controlled from the outset. In addition, they will have to monitor risks on a quantitative basis to help ensure all is going according to plan and to highlight the exceptions.

The greatest change may be triggered by e-commerce. As it is becoming more common to conduct business electronically, without ever seeing a person or having a relationship, business models and processes will be transformed. Some firms will be disintermediated out of the value chain, while others will use e-business to re-intermediate themselves at another point.

Making an explicit link between risk and strategic planning

As stated earlier, financial services firms are taking fewer market and credit risks and expanding their services in fee-based and other areas where operational risk is the major component. Therefore, operational risk becomes a strategic initiative. As a strategic initiative, it must be considered as something more than just an approach to reduce hazards. Instead, it must be considered as an opportunity, since by better understanding and managing operational risk, institutions create product and service opportunities and competitive advantage.

Balancing process and culture

The two approaches to operational risk management – process based and culture based – will become more complementary. The firms that are very process based, with formal policies, processes, measures and reporting, are likely to change their cultures and values to be more sensitive to change, provide more accountability, and expect people to do the right thing. Others that are less formal and rely on people to make the right decisions in the best interest of the firm will institute new, more formal frameworks, and procedures to deal with the influx of new people. When consistent training and experience are lacking, processes help provide the right guidance.

Both process and culture are important when it comes to effective and efficient operational risk management, because they are safety nets for each other. When the scale is tipped one way or the other, there are increased chances of people taking unwarranted risk, whether consciously or not.

Increasing focus on quantification

There will be continued effort to advance the quantitative aspects of operational risk management. Three trends are emerging: sharing of event data; more sophisticated capital models; and comprehensive and predictive indicators.

Major operational events are very rare, and internal experience alone is insufficient to truly understand and quantify the range of potential exposures. Several industry initiatives are underway to encourage organizations to share their operational risk events. While there are concerns over confidentiality and non-attribution of potentially sensitive information, there is an expectation that fears will be overcome when the value of sharing information is proven and becomes a more standard practice. There is an opportunity to record experiences inherent in individual business lines in global databases. Quantification of economic capital for operational risk will continue to advance. Current methodologies are limited by data availability, both internal and external. With better loss databases, and sharing of event data, alternate modelling approaches can be explored and validated. With more data available, models will rely on hard statistics to build accurate and dependable figures. Eventually, an internal model approach for operational risk may meet regulatory approval, as it does for market risk.

Lastly, use of indicators and escalation criteria will expand, but in a more focused fashion. Particularly for senior levels of management, indicators will evolve, leading to those few with the highest predictive power and best link to business strategy. These same indicators will be incorporated into the balanced scorecards of executive management.

While firms collect risk indicators and losses today, few link the two in a meaningful sense. While indicators are chosen with the intent to be predictive, the relationship between these indicators and actual events remains largely unproven. We will see increasing analysis of correlations between indicators, causes and consequences, making possible a better understanding of the underlying drivers of risk and predictors of where problems may occur.

Insurance programmes for operational risk will grow, if they can demonstrate true economic value. The insurance industry is increasing its service offerings in the area of operational risk. As the potential scope increases, services will be focused on risk exposures that are under the control of the institution. Firms will be faced with the question of theoretically insuring what they have the power to prevent, and in fact, the conditions of coverage may dictate that comprehensive controls be in effect.

As options for insuring operational risk grow, programmes will become more accepted, particularly for high-exposure events. These are beyond the risk appetite of any institution, and insurance in such cases becomes valuable. It will be important to reflect these insurance benefits in economic capital models, or businesses will bear a double economic burden – the insurance premium and a capital charge. By the same token, new risks often challenge the contractual language in contracts and the risks assumed to be insured might be disputed if and when an event occurs. A risk must be clearly covered and recoverable before providing a full capital benefit.

For all but the most serious consequences, it is likely that spending on internal controls is something that companies need to do anyway, and insurance coverage of the same risks is potentially a double expense. The insurance market will be most successful selling policies with very high deductibles to cover these rare events that would have a material impact on earnings.

Changes in the e-business world

Introduction

Many more organizations now consider the Internet as integral to their present and future business. E-business is transforming the way in which business is conducted between organizations, and between organizations and their customers. Businesses are realizing that the scope for e-business is much wider than they first thought and are using the Internet to effect better supply-chain management, as a means for achieving business reengineering goals, marketing, as well as reaping the benefits from on-line sales in business-to-consumer markets.

There is no doubt that the opportunities presented by the Internet are enormous. Businesses can use e-business to cut costs, cut product time to market, increase revenues through on-line sales, improve relationships with customers, promote brand awareness, and make a number of organizational efficiency gains. The growth of e-business is also fundamentally changing the ways in which businesses interact with each other, and the way in which customers interact with businesses.

However, the gold rush to exploit these opportunities, using what is still a new channel to market contains many risks. This is especially apparent in the business-to-consumer market. Much of the unmanaged risk stems from companies attempting to be 'first-timers' with their electronic commerce offerings – those that are the first to launch a web-site to capture market share before anyone else in a particular market. This has led to the phenomenon that too many web-sites are launched without a sound business model or case. One typical consequence is the continual scrapping of projects, owing to the failure to make technology sufficiently scaleable to cope with increased demand, or the lack of a strategic plan, which then throws earlier e-commerce attempts into question once new market conditions develop.

Despite the explosion of direct services and global, continuous operations, especially over the Internet, established businesses and new start-ups are experiencing highly publicized disruptions to services. These failures, which are making newspaper headlines, are having a direct impact on shareholder value, revenues, market share and the quality of customer service.

Common problems afflicting new e-businesses

- Internet banking services failing to complete thousands of banking transactions at times of peak demand. Money transferred out of accounts may not be recovered for a number of weeks.

- Software problems mean that Internet systems may be down for hours, preventing users from accessing sites and buying. Companies that have experienced such problems have, as a direct result, lost literally billions of dollars of value as the stock market has downgraded them immediately after.

- Internet servers collapsing, rendering sites useless.

- The collapse of databases under the weight of transactions at times of peak demand, creating bottlenecks in the systems when payments are delayed. Business volumes can sometimes exceed the parameters set when databases are installed.

The problems outlined in the box cannot be attributed to technology alone. There is mounting evidence to suggest that current management practices surrounding the new technology are holding organizations back from exploiting the opportunities of new Internet ventures and on-line sales, rather than facilitating success. Many on-line ventures are based on exciting new ideas and entrepreneurial drive. Indeed, many of these entrepreneurs may have extensive IT knowledge and skills. But in many Internet ventures, there can often be a wide gap between IT experience and operational management experience. The danger is that many ventures will miss out on opportunities because of a loss of management control over operations and various contingencies that may arise, and a lack of direction at the strategic level.

There are a number of operational risk issues that companies have to consider in on-line ventures. Companies may be subject to very tight implementation deadlines for marketing a new service. They may have little experience of the new technology and may not have thought through how it can be scaleable. There may be a lack of internal buy-in and strategic direction. They may not have considered properly the issue of using their own warehouse and distribution networks, or partnership with other suppliers.

Building in operational risk management practices is vital if companies are to succeed in their on-line ventures. Having noted the litany of failed business web-sites that have experienced problems and lost potential customers, many brands have been reluctant to enter into e-commerce because of the possible brand damage that may result from disruption to service. Operational risk management has a crucial role to play in safeguarding businesses from operational error and disruption. Just as important, it can provide the foundation for management to take on risk with confidence and exploit more e-business opportunities in the future.

Building trust

Businesses need to ensure that they do not waste e-business opportunities by neglecting operational issues. One solution is to ensure that enough attention is paid to preventing disruption from happening in the first place, through 'operational resilience' (first explored in Chapter 1). Simply put, operational resilience is the minimization and prevention of disruption to service. It involves the design, build, and operation of resilient service delivery and management functions, especially the management of performance, capability, demand, and stress.

In focusing on prevention rather than cure, the concept of operational resilience differs to previous risk management techniques. Whereas business continuity planning, for example, emphasizes business recovery after disruption has occurred, the focus with operational resilience is on service quality and continuous delivery. It goes beyond a concern with catastrophic events, to examine a broader range of occurrences that may lead to service disruption.

The focus with operational resilience is excellent customer service. In the modern business age, it is no longer acceptable simply to recover from failures. Due to changes in customer perceptions, and other trends, businesses cannot rely on excuses when mistakes do occur. In more competitive markets, organizations are finding that they can differentiate themselves by ensuring greater levels of trust among their customers in providing high levels of continuous service. Simply put, people will not use an e-business site unless they trust it will work. Increasingly, people expect to receive 24-hour a day, 7-day a week, 52-week, 365 days a year service.

In other words, operational resilience is more than just a focus on technology. An example that helps to explain why was a recent product launch over the Internet by a financial service provider. In the first few weeks, new customers were finding it difficult to withdraw money from their account using the new service. The problem was located not with the technology or the availability, but with the manual processes that sat behind the technology.

To think about this some more, a good example would be how an organization like Formula One operates. Leveraging the latest technology for materials in the car bodies and so on is an important component of the success of the organization. But the success of the team overall hinges on a wide range of factors. There are the mechanics in the pit lane, the designers and technicians, as well as sponsors and suppliers. In this context, focusing on the technology to ensure operational continuity would be too narrow an approach.

The need for operational resilience

Some of the key questions that businesses have to ask themselves include:

- Do we have enough operational resilience to support large increases in volume?

- How do we ensure a well-managed service when we launch a service on the Internet?

- How do we assure regulators and investors of the resilience of our on-line banking business?

- How can we minimize the number of disruptions we have been suffering?

- How do we forecast and respond to customer services demand when we re-vamp card services?

Some of the aims of operational resilience include:

- helping management to deliver service performance objectives;

- diagnosing weaknesses in service delivery processes, dependencies, and the service management function, and recommending improvements to effectiveness and efficiency;

- determining the key performance measures, stress indicators, and tolerances which need to be monitored and managed;

- designing the modelling, monitoring and reporting solution;

- designing and helping to build a best-practice service management function; and

- implementing successful change through world-class project management.

Examples of existing operational resilience

There are many good examples of organizations that already have strong operational resilience. For instance, people have come to rely on an instant dialling tone when picking up a telephone, a continuity of service which is backed up by high levels of stability in telecommunications networks. Similarly, many sources of power are continuous. Power cuts occasionally happen, perhaps in extreme weather conditions, but for most of the time society has become reliant on continuous electricity in homes and offices.

- The National Grid in the United Kingdom copes with really peaky consumer electricity demand, often in short sharp bursts like half time in the World Cup final.

- BT closely monitors network performance at its complex Oswestry Operations Centre, and is able to respond to peaks in demand such as those caused by TV show phone-ins.

- Premier IT services providers such as IBM (Warwick) and EDS (Stockley Park) have major operational management centres maintaining service delivery quality.

- Some financial service providers have operated disruption-free services for many years, especially those providing third-party services such as clearing and settlement.

Organizations that have long histories of delivering public utilities, or services that experience cyclical and rapidly fluctuating demand, may be considered good-practice models. Organizations that have learned from their experiences in delivering steady services tend to manage operations better than start-ups or those launching new ventures, often because initial performance is over-estimated, demand and customer behaviour is unknown, and so the sizing of required capacity of systems, customer service and call centre functions is extremely difficult. Businesses that build from previous experience, run pilots and launch services or access new markets incrementally tend to prove more resilient.

While these organizations do achieve a high level of operational continuity and stability, they also highlight the extra challenges associated with e-business. Utilities for example have spent perhaps decades building up knowledge of operational processes and procedures, while new businesses set up in shorter time spans cannot rely on this amount of time and build-up of knowledge to develop operational responses as circumstances unfold.

Underestimating demand and capacity planning

One of the main reasons for web-site failure to date has been the tendency for companies to underestimate on-line demand. Following the launch of a site, servers have collapsed due to the number of hits a web-site receives, leading to the collapse of the web-site. Many web-sites are built to cope with only a limited number of users. When millions of extra people attempt to access the site, it can crash, leading to access problems for days after. For example, one site that crashed estimated a top limit of 25 million requests a day, and received 50 million requests an hour when it launched. The consequence of such a disruption to service is poor image in the marketplace as millions of disillusioned customers wonder whether it is worth returning to the site again.

Busy periods such as Christmas are likely to test e-commerce sites often for the first time. Web-site failures and slow response times from over-loaded servers during holiday seasons in the last few years have led to lost sales and dissatisfied customers. In the worse case scenario, the credibility and reputation of an organization as a whole has been affected. Underestimating demand is a critical question as the opposite scenario – overestimating demand – may turn out to be an equally large problem. Companies may be burdened with an expensive IT infrastructure that is being under-utilized.

The problem of demand management is compounded because of the particular difficulty in forecasting demand with on-line response and sales. With traditional businesses in various industries, there is a range of indicators to show future demand, such as seasonal behaviour or particular economic cycles. Such indicators do not apply where e-business is concerned, however. The question of predicting demand is perhaps easier in Europe and other markets, where the experience of web-site launches in the US can be used as a benchmark for launching in Europe. There are, in addition, a range of forecasts for Internet access and other data sources that can be used. A demand comparison can be made with the equivalent market off-line to estimate how much money is spent on a good, how quickly goods are sold and in what numbers, and so on. Finally, there are technological solutions. One common solution is 'mirroring', which entails the provision of back-up servers in case of crashes. Another is the flexible buying of extra bandwidth as it is needed on a case-by-case basis.

Web-site launches

There are a whole host of operational issues that organizations with new Internet ventures have to consider. The following examples illustrate actual mistakes that have been made in the last few years with web-site launches.

- Many companies have made the mistake of informing the press of a launch before their systems are live. This then increases the amount of pressure on them when launch dates are continually put back. The result is that customers are even more expectant of good service, and, consequently, more willing to abandon the web-site if something else goes wrong.

- Experience has shown that there is a need for those running e-business services to react quickly to short-term indicators. This is important from a business strategy perspective, because the horizon or window in which management has to react is that much shorter. While every month, a business in heavy industry may have a planning meeting, for e-business it could be a meeting to change its whole strategy.

- The same rules that businesses abide by in their normal operations are often thrown out of the window in the context of e-business. For example, most businesses carry out market research, hold focus groups, and gain customer feedback when launching a new product. However, there is evidence to suggest that much of this process is being by-passed with the Internet as organizations attempt to be first to tap into a new on-line market.

- There may be too much of a reliance on the design and the front look of a web-site, at the expense of back-end security and stability. While attractive designs will please potential customers, the lack of stability or resources to cope with potential disruptions to service is far more likely to lead to permanently lost customers. While many have identified the problem with e-business failure as being insufficient market spend, the problem is equally one of ensuring the system works and, most importantly, being able to meet customer expectations convincingly and comprehensively when launching and delivering a new service on-line. This means having a more realistic appraisal of fixing dates for product launches.

- Organizations can run into problems when they try to guarantee a high degree of customer service without back-up or resources. Many companies have claimed they will offer a next-day delivery guarantee while underestimating the resources required to carry out that kind of service. A similar problem is that e-mail enquiries from a web-site go unanswered or there is a poor response time, leading quickly to dissatisfied customers.

- When launching a new Internet venture, organizations need to create successful 'on-line communities' which mean that consumers are far more likely to return again and again. The best examples in this category tend to have a high level of interactivity (such as getting customers to contribute to the web-site, book reviews being the classic example). Other portal sites have a high level of participation and are successful as a result. A portal site is a web-site that aims to be a 'doorway' to the world-wide web, typically offering a search engine and/or links to useful pages, and possibly news and other services. These services are usually provided for free in the hope that users will make the site their default home page or at least will visit it often. Most portals exist to generate advertising income for their owners.

- As e-business becomes a single delivery channel, there are greater costs associated with e-business failure. This is partly because of the medium itself. For example, human resources are on standby in a bank branch if anything goes wrong. With e-business, however, that option is not open. The cost of failure also increases because of the ease in which consumers can access services. The customer is more in control, but that means they have more scope to get things wrong.

The operational resilience envelope

The concept of the operational resilience envelope (see Figure 4.2) is to create a protective cover over particular processes and departments in order to pre-empt the possibility of disruption. It attempts to address typical operational e-business issues from an integrated perspective involving:

● business drivers;

● performance obligations;

● business processes;

● stress indicators; and

● managing service.

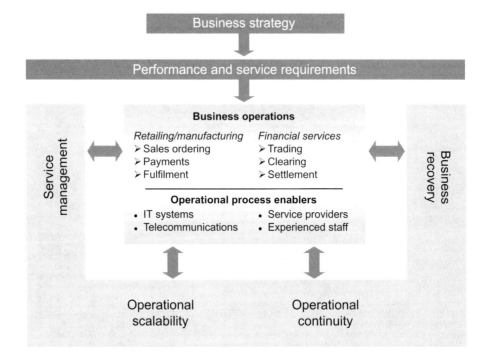

Figure 4.2 Wrapping an operational resilience envelope around business operations

Business drivers

Before launching an electronic commerce offering, organizations need to examine their wider, strategic perspectives. Among the key questions to be asked are:

● what service do we require; and

● how do we develop it?

These help to clarify the overall picture. An important component is taking into account, and planning for, changes in strategy. To what extent will existing business processes and technology support a change in strategy six months down the line?

Performance obligations

This estimates the resources required to deliver a service. Obligations fall into: time-based (availability); cost-based (the cost of transactions); and quality (for example, can the customer access other web-sites from a site?). This category also covers obligations to shareholders, stakeholders, and suppliers. One group often ignored is regulators.

Business processes

This stage is most closely related to risk assessment. Questions to ask include:

● What are planned?

● What processes exist?

● What are the risks and dependencies associated with change?

Critical areas to examine include: staff, technical support, suppliers, plants and equipment.

One central issue is to ask the question, again, of speed and model changes. The fact that process change in a dynamic, e-business environment will be a part of normal day-to-day operations should be built into processes at the design stage.

Stress indicators

This takes the 'prevention rather than cure' approach further. Defining stress indicators may include staff turnover or sickness, or the number of calls per hour in a call centre. Similarly, tolerances need to be defined. If a normal baseline is fifty calls per hour, then it may be the case that a business can operate within certain boundaries, say between forty and fifty-five calls per hour. At forty calls per hour, the company may still make a profit. But outside of these thresholds, the company might have to take action to prevent operational stress. The key is to generate information about staff turnover, on a daily, hourly, or annual basis. This information can be used to inform management that action at some point in the future will be required.

A central point is that these indicators are needed precisely because of the difficulties in predicting demand. Most bank branches can predict with some accuracy how many customers they will receive on a Monday morning, based on past experience. This option is not open to e-businesses. This issue can be overcome by using an approach which may be characterized as 'taking the pulse' of a business. By measuring factors such as transaction volumes, and how many rings it takes for people to answer a phone, managers can build up a better overview of operational stress points.

Managing service

A range of functions exists to ensure continuous service. Most of these functions are not new and many of them are not best adapted to changes in business models. As business models change, so too do functions. The most important consideration is factoring in dynamic change into models. Organizations may have not asked whether these functions will be capable of delivering service in two years', or a number of years' time.

Conclusion

Successful implementation of operational resilience should lead to the following key indicators of success:

- organization focused on customer service quality as a priority;

- high value placed on quality people management;

- culture – blaming the unexpected no longer acceptable;

- active and pervasive risk management;

- supplier alignment;

- integration between front desk and back office;

- highly scaleable services – quickly factor up and down;

- integration between service management functions;

- control and successful management of change;

- intelligent long-term demand modelling and forecasting;

- acute understanding of stress indicators and tolerances; and

- rapid management of short-term demand and performance.

Case study: the launch of a pharmaceuticals web-site

A new web-site launched for a pharmaceuticals company, selling medical products on-line, is a good example of the potential rewards but also the high risks involved with on-line ventures. Off-line pharmacies have to ensure a high level of supervision to protect the health of customers. For example, certain products cannot be consumed if the patient is already taking other forms of medication. However, on-line environments take away the human dimension. As a result, some web-sites have adopted an alert system so that consumers' medical conditions can be correlated and dangers avoided. There is even a case that web-sites may be safer, as more comprehensive medical records and databases can be constructed behind the web-site, gathering more information each time customers buy products.

Risk and restructuring

Shared service centres

Around 40 per cent of Fortune 500 companies now have some shared services groups, compared to around 20 per cent three or four years ago. In the European context, shared services centres (SSC) are becoming more common. An SSC allows a corporation to bring together and integrate similar internal service functions and business processes that may exist in dispersed form across an organization. These may include finance and accounting processes – such as accounts payable and accounts receivable processes – as well as distribution, human resource management, purchasing and information technology support processes.

A number of objectives underpin the establishment of SSCs. The main aim is to reduce overheads, eliminate duplication and provide a more efficient level of service, not through centralization, but through the running of a centre as a separate, stand-alone business which is subject to market forces and performance requirements. For example, they may be competing with external professional service providers for the business of the parent organization, and similarly, may be serving markets outside of the parent organization.

SSCs can also reduce the amount of management time in running what are essentially support functions in an organization. They can help to bring a consistency to processes, practices, definitions and codes. They also offer the opportunity for organizations to reengineer functions and processes afresh, often around industry best practices. Businesses can make organization and system changes at the same time, for example. Overall, the objective is to generate value from what was previously an internal function.

In Europe, many pan-European organizations still have a separate organizational structure in each country in which they operate. Cross-cultural differences, cross-border communication barriers and the lack of a single European currency have served as obstacles to many businesses setting up an SSC. The European Union (EU) still remains fragmented on a country-by-country basis, in terms of differences between laws, accounting practices, tax rules, employment legislation, and currency. However, improvements in cross-border communication services – such as video conferencing, voice and data communication links – and the move towards a single European currency, are now focusing management attention on the benefits of European SSCs. These centres have an important role to play in enabling organizations to achieve key business objectives of controlling costs and improving return on capital.

Many successful businesses have already relocated processes to national or regional SSCs. Some of the quantifiable benefits they provide include:

● elimination of duplicate activities across different departments and different countries/subsidiaries;

- creation of economies of scale and the achievement of sub-sequent reductions in overall headcount;

- standardization of processes, practices, definitions and codes; and

- availability of comparable, timely pan-European perform-ance data for benchmarking.

In addition to these quantifiable benefits, there is a range of intangible factors that an SSC contributes to an organization. Some of the softer benefits that arise from consolidation of finance and accounting functions, for example, relate to improvements in service, support and flexibility provided to the business.

Such benefits include:

- long-term improved morale and career path for finance and other support staff;

- business management in each location freed from responsi-bility of managing support processes;

- facilitation of similar change in other areas (e.g. logistics); and

- reduction in cost and complexity of subsequent change initiatives.

SSC risks

SSC initiatives tend to cross many boundaries – functional, process, geographic, regional, national, cultural – and conse-quently, are often very complex. They tend to involve multiple, concurrent projects, especially as the migration stage approaches. Setting up an SSC is a large-scale change manage-ment initiative and can be very disruptive. It is a high-risk activity where risks are commensurate with rewards.

The early identification of potential problems, through risk evaluation, monitoring and reporting, helps the programme management team make resource allocation decisions so that a minor issue does not develop into a major incident. Proactive risk management should play an essential part in the management decision making process from the outset of the change programme.

A risk management framework should cover:

- **strategy:** risk management policies, objectives, and performance drivers;

- **risk management processes:** awareness, assessment, improvement and reporting;

- **infrastructure:** people, systems and tools; and

- **environment:** culture, third parties, regulators, legislators.

Alongside operational risk management, key issues to remember include:

- A strong programme management infrastructure helps minimize the impact of this disruption and maximizes the likelihood of early successes.

- Senior management's total commitment to the establishment of an SSC is needed to maximize the value that the programme will bring.

- The inclusion of internal and external audit at an early stage in the change programme helps foster a good working relationship that will assist management and minimize the potentially disruptive impact of multiple teams of auditors on the progress of the programme itself.

Evaluating the risks of different options

There are a number of 'routes' that businesses can take in establishing an SSC. All of these carry different kinds of risks and rewards. The main routes, using the example of the different ways in which the IT function can be consolidated, may be considered as:

Route A

A business makes an organization and system change simultaneously. This means that there is only one change required, in one quick move. There is only one lot of knowledge transfer. There is a better chance of achieving best practice because of the high level of change in organizational culture.

Main risks: Not all the benefits will feed through immediately to the parent organization. Initially, there may be a drop in service as new processes start on day one, and post-implementation, there may be a degree of fire fighting. There are usually very high (and often enormous) investments in capital and people. There are a variety of changes that cannot be anticipated at the planning stage and there is always the risk of delay as functions and the core business need to be aligned.

Route B

There is a migration to an SSC on existing, legacy systems and then a move to implement new systems in the SSC. The change is tackled in manageable chunks, therefore removing risk. Demands made on senior management may be flexible and management may be less diverted from running the core business.

Main risks: Two sets of changes are required step-by-step; achieving the final goal may take a longer time. For the interim period, the SSC remains the prisoner of the legacy systems. There may be a problem with internal buy-in at the senior management level compared with Route A, where there is a more immediate change with more tangible and immediate benefits.

Route C

An implementation of a common technology platform is made, which is then consolidated in an SSC. This offers lower complexity and risk than Route A, and there is greater scope for flexibility when it comes to structuring the final form of the SSC.

Main risks: Human capital may be lost as trained staff may leave when the SSC is implemented. The costs are heavily weighted towards the front end of the project. Until the SSC is implemented, the platform may not support new organization models.

Route D
The SSC idea is abandoned and it is chosen to outsource the function. This may offer the business a greater focus on core competencies, 'guaranteed' savings and early benefits.

Main risks: Any outsourcing project involves a potential loss of knowledge, as well as a loss of control and loss of flexibility. Additionally, the possibility of unrest among disgruntled staff is increased, as there is a greater change in employment structures. Finally, the outsourcing vendor takes a margin from running the function, a charge that does not take place under a SSC.

Critical success factors

The establishment of a successful shared service centre depends on a number of critical success factors that include:

- The authority and commitment of the management team. The appointment of a leader with proven credibility to run the overall change programme is necessary. There should also be a clear hand-over of authority from this individual to the SSC manager as the centre approaches operational readiness. Long-term commitment from senior management is required if the shared service centre is to add value to the rest of the organization.

- Effective and timely communications and internal public relations. The planning phase of an SSC can be tense. Operating units are faced with uncertainties regarding future responsibilities and staff in their control. Staff need to be informed about change and the impact of the SSC.

- Human resource management. HR management is perhaps the most critical factor of all, particularly when employees are unwilling to travel or relocate to other countries. Clear redundancy, retention and recruitment plans are critical.

- Rigorous process design, integration, and optimization. The redesign and standardization of processes to be moved to the SSC is crucial to the success or failure of the SSC. End-to-end checks and controls should be built into the design process.

- Strong and consistent programme management. The creation of a pan-European SSC (or a series of regional centres) is a major change programme in its own right and like all such programmes, requires rigorous and consistent management focus over an extended period of time.

- Understanding of cross-cultural and cross-border issues. When relocating processes into an SSC, management's ability to recognize and address the cross-cultural challenges is an important factor. These challenges may range from language differences, to social legislation differences in each country, tax, and legal issues, local policies and procedures, different statutory reporting requirements, the impact of a single European currency and the fact that public holidays are taken on different dates across Europe.

- Managing stakeholder needs. It is important that stakeholders' needs – often conflicting – are recognized and met. For example, client management may seek to reduce costs, usually by reducing headcount; but employees may need to feel secure to give their full co-operation to the transition process. There is also a need to eliminate duplication of activities across locations, especially across increasingly global operations, while ensuring that tax and regulatory requirements in each country are met.

Life cycle of a programme to establish an SSC

- **Stage One: Developing the business case for change.** A business case supporting the establishment of a SCC is prepared in a format that will guide senior management through the investment appraisal process.

- **Stage Two: Transition planning.** The scope of the services to be provided by the SSC is confirmed, SSC management and support infrastructure requirements are defined, and a conceptual model of the optimized processes to be relocated to the SSC prepared.

- **Stage Three: Transition.** The SSC management team is established and builds the infrastructure needed to support the processes to be moved to the SSC. Systems and telecommunications services are selected and implemented. Interfaces are built and data prepared for migration. SSC staff are recruited and trained. Premises are located and prepared. Suppliers of services needed to support the SSC are identified and contractual relationships established. SSC staff start to take over operational process responsibilities in each location. In parallel with the activities, 'as is' process knowledge is gathered. This information is used to design and implement the optimized processes to be operated in the SSC.

- **Stage Four: Migration.** The processes and SSC staff are moved from their country locations to the SSC when all acceptance testing has been successfully completed and all 'go live' criteria have been met.

- **Stage Five: On-going operations.** As the SCC nears steady state, the establishment programme is wound down and management control of the processes is migrated to the SSC management team. SSC management's responsibilities include implementing a continuous improvement programme tasked with ensuring that the level of the service provided by the SSC meets or exceeds client management's expectations.

Developing the business case for change

Define objectives

These may include cost reductions, standardization, the modernizing of the workforce and the rationalization of existing processes.

Assess current environment

Organizations need to understand the current environment in each location by assessing processes, competencies, culture, systems, facilities, and tax and legal obligations. The objective of this assessment is to develop a business case for change that provides senior management with the information needed to make a decision whether or not to implement an SSC. The decision is based on a number of criteria including cost and performance, qualitative factors (such as the learning possible through co-location of finance expertise), and the impact of an SSC on people, culture, business processes, systems, telecommunication services, facilities, infrastructure, as well as global tax and regulatory issues. Senior management should understand the projected shareholder value and cost reduction benefits from the SSC.

Each process that is to be migrated to the SSC in each location needs to be assessed, and different scenarios evaluated with the objective of identifying the scenarios that offer the best overall cost benefit. The information gathered will provide a means for evaluating the impact of the change on people, processes, systems and facilities, and for estimating likely costs, savings and other benefits. A proposed SSC management structure can be developed which sets out proposed roles and responsibilities. A cost allocation model in which charge back policies are described can be also developed, to model the financial impact of the SCC on cash flows for both client and SSC management.

Risk assessment, of tax and legal risks, as well as an investment risk appraisal, is critical to this stage. Management should consider transition project planning and initiate a programme risk assessment that highlights critical dependencies on resources, including people, systems, interfaces, premises, data and telecommunication services. The resulting implications of this assessment should be considered in terms of the potential impact on the success of the programme and estimated time-scales for each phase of the SSC implementation.

Define scope of services

The case for change will define – at a high level – the scope of services to be provided and the locations to be served by an SSC. The definition of scope of services should also describe the boundaries between the processes to remain with the client and those to be migrated to an SSC.

Prepare business case for change

This stage represents the finalization of the business case. It involves bringing all of these elements together in a form that can be presented to executive management so that an appraisal of the overall case for change can be made.

Establish programme management

The programme management infrastructure covers all aspects of the SSC establishment and may include a programme support function responsible for co-ordinating the scheduling, common procedures and working practices, standards, methods, administration, and finance management, as well as resource planning and allocation. The programme support function will facilitate communication and help ensure that individual project streams co-ordinate with each other.

Perform due diligence reviews in each location

This is necessary to minimize migration risks. Due diligence reviews are carried out at each location to establish an understanding of the current status of the processes to be migrated to an SSC. The scope of these reviews should cover an evaluation of the adequacy of processes, the quantification of any backlogs and other programmes, adequacy of policies, procedures and controls, and current performance levels. The results of a due diligence review also provide a benchmark against which performance improvements can be measured.

Define SSC management requirements and begin establishing SSC management

After defining the services to be provided, the next step is to define the structure and organization of an SSC. Roles and responsibilities are defined and an executive search and selection for SSC management team initiated. Specialist tax and legal advice is obtained to ensure that any tax or legal issues or opportunities are identified and resolved.

Define processes to be moved to the SSC

This involves due diligence exercises to gather the information to set service level targets in service level agreements. 'Go live' criteria and milestones for each phase are defined and resources allocated to capture them. Research is also carried out to collect and collate existing process policies so that SSC process policies can be defined.

Define SCC infrastructure requirements and begin establishing SSC infrastructure

Having defined the resources needed to support the processes being migrated to the SSC (people, systems, facilities, and premises), steps are taken to identify and select the most appropriate implementation strategies. These will typically cover:

- systems and telecommunications services;

- human resource planning and recruitment;

- premises logistics; and

- vendor and supplier integration.

This stage also involves the establishment of a business continuity-planning project for the SCC. The objective is to ensure that the processes migrated to the SSC will continue to perform within service levels agreed with the client, in the event of a major incident.

Joint ventures

Strategic alliances and joint ventures have become popular alternatives to mergers or acquisitions, especially when both parties have identified short-term opportunities to capitalize on alternative, or mutually reinforcing, strengths. They are increasingly taking place as businesses take advantage of networked resources, in the context of freer associations between previously separate companies. Typically, strategic alliances and joint ventures benefit parties because a working relationship can add up to something greater than its constituent parts.

However, while joint ventures allow greater flexibility than, say a merger, there is a danger that the source of this advantage can become an exposure to risk; that business relationships, driven by short-term and flexible considerations, will become too opportunistic and backfire.

The risk-reward equation, therefore, is starkly outlined. On the one hand, the potential for maximizing return is potentially enlarged. Companies have potential access to a wider range of markets, for example, and may be able to guarantee more success in launching a new product. The main risk is that

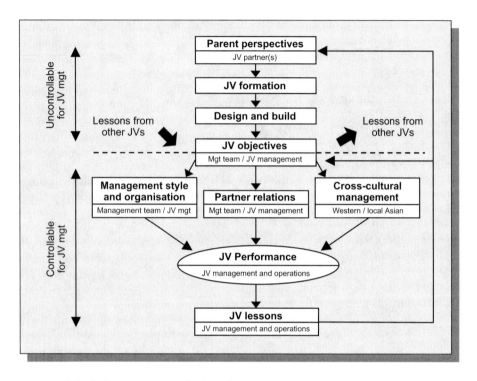

Figure 4.3 Joint venture relationships

a number of problem areas could become magnified, and prevent the venture from pursuing opportunities. By anticipating contingencies, the aim of risk management should be to ensure that potential problems are anticipated and that rewards are safeguarded.

The key is first making a conscious decision to accept and manage risk at the strategy formation stage. The second requirement is to anticipate the shape of risk management once the venture gets off the ground. An effective risk management strategy must be careful not to stifle the venture with too many compliance requirements in the early stages. There will be a pressure to go to market that may involve a high degree of risk taking activity. At the same time, management has to be armed with knowledge of potential risks that can arise.

As joint ventures involve relationships between parties, operational risk management should take a different form to its practice within a single organization. Risk management processes should evolve over time to suit the particular culture and needs of the relationship. Market circumstances will change and the joint venture or strategic alliance, and the management of risk must keep pace. Both sides need to remain flexible and be prepared to return to evaluate risk management practices as the relationship matures and new circumstances arise.

Key risk areas

The key risk areas in any joint venture are threefold:

- cultural;
- financial; and
- geographical.

Cultural compatibility is a prerequisite to the success of any organizational marriage. Parties need to assess the risk appetite and risk tolerance of the other. A relationship that brings together a risk taking organization with one that is risk averse is unlikely to foster a coherent approach to market opportunities. An assessment of possible cultural differences often takes place on the basis of gut feel. Risk behaviour, for example, is not something that can be regimented too strictly. The decision to embark upon a joint venture may be based on emotional grounds anyway – building on, for example, a successful interpersonal working relationship.

The category of *financial* risk involves anticipating the financial stability of the proposed partner. The key factor is not to make any assumptions about present or future financial circumstances. This may also include an assessment of liabilities that may be impending which have a bearing on the partnership in the future. There is a danger that risk management will stop once financial due diligence has been carried out: the main risks may lie in how combined services are to be delivered in future. This category, therefore, also includes the risk that service levels of one party or another will alter from their expected course, which could lead directly to a financial loss and possible loss of reputation. Service level agreements may need to be clarified at the outset, with a degree of flexibility built in to accommodate changing circumstances.

Geographical risk mainly addresses fluctuations in geographical markets and industries in overseas economies. This risk may be political, economic or financial in nature.

Other key risk considerations are:

- Both parties need to be practical in their approach. It is important to remember that risk management is supplementary to the business process, and should facilitate, not stifle, business opportunities.

- Too many potential, or existing, joint venture partners assume that their commitment to putting a legal agreement in place is the most important risk management initiative. This is not the case. Relationships of trust, which relate to cultural factors – see above – may be more important to the success of the venture. The legal agreement is the last resort and, ideally, neither party should have to rely on the contract to allocate the responsibility and liability for any risk encountered and its impact. A related consideration is that the contract should not increase the risk of a dispute by the way it is worded.

- It is important to discuss fully the fee-sharing arrangements, working methods and suitability of staff for any projects under consideration.

- It may make sense to conduct due diligence into the quality of staff in the proposed partner, and devote time and resources to ensuring full compatibility between all IT and communications systems.

Mergers and acquisitions

Mergers and acquisitions (M&As) have become a familiar feature of the current business landscape. However, it is well known that a large proportion of mergers and acquisitions – maybe as much as 30 per cent – do not achieve their objectives, in terms of growth in earnings, perceived operational synergies, new product development, management stability and share price performance. Unanticipated stumbling blocks can appear halfway through the process, taking everyone by surprise.

The key objective of any due diligence process is the need to reduce the likelihood that hidden surprises, with a material impact on the value of the business, are identified after the deal is struck. However, due diligence procedures tend to focus narrowly on evaluation of historic financial performance and future profit projections and often neglect wider operational issues. Even when a wider scope of the due diligence is undertaken this is often limited to an assessment of tax, market due diligence and IT. The danger can be that businesses are wrongly valued and buyers face unanticipated operational problems after acquiring a company. Wider business trends are prompting consideration of operational issues at the due diligence stage. Interestingly, an upside of the Y2K millennium bug has focused attention on the importance of IT and operations as a key enabler of business success, and therefore the need to assess the effectiveness of IT systems, management information and operations. As the market in buying and selling companies continues to boom, equity providers investing in new start-up businesses, particularly those focusing on technology, require greater assurances that companies will be managed securely.

As an analogy to the way in which many acquisitions are undertaken today, take the process of purchasing a second-hand car. Focusing only on a narrow range of factors such as book price, service history and a cursory glance under the bonnet and kick of the tyres relies to a large extent on gut feeling, experience and luck! A more prudent approach would be to:

● obtain an independent assessment of the car from an expert in car mechanics;

● carry out a search to establish ownership and the right to sell; and

● test drive the vehicle, etc.

Clearly a more 'holistic' approach to the buying process is likely to reduce the likelihood of hidden surprises down stream.

'Placing a value' on operational risks at the due diligence stage is the logical starting point. Such an approach requires the identification of key business processes and the dependencies that support them. By widening the scope of due diligence, bidders and potential business partners can gain a strategic view of a target organization's core operational strengths and weaknesses.

There are a number of reasons why this approach is not widely adopted, however. Personnel involved at the due diligence stage may not fully understand what a purchaser or partner is looking for. Reports on the status of operations for example often delve deeply into technical material but may provide little information of relevance to the buyer's needs. Although staff may have the right technical skill sets, they may communicate an operational rather than strategic view of particular processes and systems. One message of this book, however, is that operational risk assessment and strategy must go hand in hand.

An operational due diligence process aims to identify and assess the impact to the value of the transaction of operational issues arising from mergers and acquisitions. Its main objectives are to:

- identify key business processes and extent of reliance on third parties that enable the service or operations to be delivered on schedule;

- identify the controls and management activities that ensure the operational integrity of the processes; and

- assess the fit of current activities to the changed environment and resolve any mismatches.

The scope must include all business enablers that support the organizations. These may be:

- management information;

- key staff, particularly those who are the main knowledge conduits between processes;

- the relative importance of physical assets of all types;

- the frameworks which structure the processes, be they legal agreements, accounting rules, standards or procedures;

- the use of third parties; and

- dependency on assumptions relating to the use of technology.

It is critical that the following risks are assessed during due diligence so that they can be addressed as early as possible in the integration process.

Management information

Is the Management Information sufficient to run the business?

A key aspect relating to management's ability to make informed decisions about the future direction of the business is the availability of timely, complete and accurate management information. Many organizations continue to focus on a narrow set of financial indicators such as EBITDA (earnings before tax depreciation and assets), return on investment and cash flow. While these are clearly important, other indicators may also be relevant, including information relating to operational performance, customer service, quality, product reliability, market and product, actual verses target, capacity etc.

Failure to identify and monitor an appropriate set of key performance indicators that are linked to the business strategy is a key weakness in many organizations today. The equivalent would be sailing in an ocean liner in the North Atlantic relying only on the position of the stars to guide you safely to your destination.

An evaluation of the usefulness of existing management information systems (MIS) is often critical for private equity providers acquiring high growth, hi-tech small organizations. In many instances, the information actually provided is incomplete, out of date, and in some cases misleading.

Typical concerns include:

- The appropriateness of management information. Poorly defined key performance indicators can lead to wrong business decisions.

- Accuracy of management information. Managers will have basic problems managing the business without accurate and relevant information.

- Timeliness of management information. Without prompt closing of monthly information, action can be delayed, and without flash results available, information may be losing its value.

- The adequacy of forward looking MIS. Poor management of order book/working capital leads to funding problems in geared companies, for example.

- The cost-effective production of MIS. This involves issues such as, can information be produced more effectively, and is all the information presented relevant?

Knowledge of key people

There is a risk that only a few key individuals hold positions that are either at the organizational centre of several information flows or are responsible for a critical process that is invariably not well documented. These people must be identified quickly and either retained via some type of golden handcuff or have a minder assigned to try to learn as much as possible. This is one of the hardest risks to mitigate and often is only resolved financially.

Hidden dependencies

This usually arises where some aspect of the operational process is dependent on a third party. The most common problems arising recently are:

- dependencies on shared services, such as in-sourced or out-sourced IT, financial process, HR process and call centres;

- dependencies on group functions such as Treasury, consolidated reporting, legal, tax, regulatory compliance;

- dependencies on shared infrastructure, buildings, telecommunications, IT; and

- contracts and licences tied to a specific entity that may not be transferable.

The cost and impact of merging separate organizations needs to take account of the fit of the senior management team in each organization, among other things. A number of recent mergers have hinged on key figures within each organization, for example Vodaphone Air touch and Mannesmann, SmithKline Beecham and Wellcome. Also, the cost associated with harmonizing working practices, including brand, marketing, customer facing processes, infrastructure, and operations needs to be taken into consideration.

Merging operational integrity frameworks and working practices

Each organization has different working practices, regardless of industry sector, but merging those practices is often only considered at a superficial level. In order to achieve cost savings, business processes will often require redesign to reduce duplication of support and management processes.

Clashes of organizational culture

This category addresses the merging of different operating cultures. As interactions between people are unpredictable, cultural integration can be difficult. Typically, there remains an association to the previous organizational structure and maintenance of the previous social networks.

Examining the extent to which management is task or people focused often reveals a great deal about the nature of an organization's culture.

Common reasons why M&As fail

- Communication to stakeholders during the due diligence stage can break down.

- Regulatory constraints can surprise organizations.

- The benefits of a transaction can be overestimated.

- Key staff can leave either party.

- Misunderstanding operational potential.

Appropriateness of information systems

Businesses are increasingly dependent on information systems. In terms of M&As, the key issues and risks faced include:

- hidden costs associated with IT systems, including the costs of conversion, integration and interfacing to make systems compatible, as well as the integration of business processes that accompany IT systems. This issue can become complicated if an organization has pursued a growth strategy through acquisition, or if systems have become heavily customized for any one particular organization;

- over dependency on a 'rump' company which may be bought by a competitor; and

- loss of expertise.

Dependence on technology

Many organizations are dependent on technology either as a means of revenue generation or as a method of achieving competitive advantage. Some current examples are:

- The Internet, which has reduced entry barriers to competitors in a number of industry sectors. For example retail banking, where competitor e-banking offerings are being introduced without the cost overhead of operating a network of branches. The Internet also provides an opportunity to bypass traditional distribution methods allowing direct access to the end customer.

- Advances in IT and telecommunications 'bandwidth' allowing high volumes of data to be transmitted. However, the realization is some way off the reality. The next three to five years, for example, will see video on demand, which effectively provides replacement technology for existing video outlets. The Time Warner/AOL merger created an opportunity to download video to around 50 per cent of the Cable TV network (owned by Time Warner) in the US.

- Introduction of WAP (wireless application protocol) mobile technology allowing Internet access from mobile phones potentially replacing existing methods of accessing the Internet.

- The current '.com boom' which sees Internet start-up companies, which may never have achieved a profit, and which often have management teams without a proven track record valued on the perceived future potential of an idea.

Clearly an approach based on valuing these companies on multiples of EBITDA is not adequate. A more holistic approach is required which considers:

- entry barriers to competition;

- risk of replacement technologies;

- resilience, quality and reliability of the service offering;

- quality of the management team;

- alliances with third parties such as web design companies and Internet service providers (ISPs);

- ability effectively to measure and monitor usage;

- usage of the application; and

- capacity to grow to meet future needs.

Carve-out separation issues

Organizations have to ensure continuity of business both during and after an M&A transaction. This will entail formulating a transition plan, comprised of:

- an estimate of total transition costs, how costs are borne by each party, and how costs are accounted for in the business plan;

- identifying the services to be provided to the buyer over a defined time-scale;

- establishing a formal contract and service level agreement to ensure the effective delivery of services. Clauses should cover: change management, management reporting of services achieved, penalties for failure to deliver service, termination of service, responsibilities of each party.

Other areas to be considered may include:

- shared network and telecommunications infrastructure;

- e-business including Internet access, web sites, EDI;

- e-mail;

- shared call centres and shared source centres, financial and other processes;

- outsourced information systems;

- consolidated group reporting;

- desktop support;

- human resources, tax, legal, compliance, internal audit;

- shared technical and research resources;

- licence costs;

- payroll;

- shared offices, plant and equipment;

- in-house developed applications; and

- shared order fulfilment, warehousing and distribution processes.

Case study: A UK leisure organization

A major organization in the UK leisure sector and a technology company producing hi-tech entertainment machines wanted to partner in a project to roll out a remote management system for games machines at leisure sites across the UK. Through the introduction of machines that would be connected to a central network, the service provider would be able to monitor sales from a centralized location, as well as offer a number of new services to the benefit of the leisure organization.

A technical review was commissioned to examine:

- Functionality requirements were in place and any limitations in the underlying design of the network identified.

- The flexibility of the system to cope with likely future terminal requirements. For example, have industry standards been adopted? Does the dial-up network provide the bandwidth for the downloading of large software files? Have resources been identified with regards to future upgrade costs?

- Technical alternatives that may be cheaper or more efficient.

- The technical capability of the provider to support and further develop the new technology across a range of other sites. For example, there may only be limited documentation of the system; formal testing procedures may not be used; there may be a danger that a critical specification is overlooked or not adequately tested; project management may be undertaken on an ad hoc basis; and a rapid development approach may result in problems going unnoticed. Management processes that may need to be adopted may include:
  - project planning, with milestones and deliverables;
  - project resource planning;
  - change management;
  - issue management;
  - test planning;
  - regular reporting; and
  - documentation.

- The critical dependencies of the provider on key personnel and third parties. For example, is there over-reliance on the designer of the software and hardware components? If that person left the organization, would his/her team leave as well? How is that person compensated within the company?

Case study: A manufacturing company

In a carve-out of a division of a multinational communications manufacturing company the acquiring company identified a number of key opportunities to build a stronger European presence by acquiring a competing manufacturer.

During the due diligence process senior management from various parts of the business formed multi-disciplinary teams bringing in external advisors to fulfil specific roles in the acquisition process such as:

- tax experts;

- operation and systems experts;

- finance and human resources; and

- operations and supply chain.

The due diligence process identified a number of critical dependencies:

- reliance on the 'rump', parent company for support and roll-out of a project to implement an enterprise resource planning (ERP) business system;

- costs associated with separating shared voice and data network and electronic mail;

- reliance on shared, centrally managed payroll services;

- central treasury; and

- consolidated management reporting.

> The due diligence team were able to quantify the risks associated with the transition process and carried out more detailed reviews of each location which involved:
>
> - identifying a reduced level of support than indicated by the target's own IT team. Reducing proposed transition support costs from over £1 million to under £200,000;
>
> - a decision to postpone implementation of the ERP project in a number of business units saving £500k; and
>
> - the need to put in place formal contracts and service-level agreements with the 'rump' for services to be provided during a six-month transition period.

Corporate governance pressures

The primary aim of the Turnbull committee is to ensure that corporate risk management becomes an integrated management process rather than an isolated year-end exercise. The spirit of the committee's guidance is that risk management should be used to help businesses achieve their key objectives. The scope of the guidance is broader than that of the previous Cadbury guidance, in that the review procedures must cover business, operational, and compliance as well as financial control.

The main challenges with the guidance are:

- The identification and management of risk should be linked to achievement of business objectives and the enhancement of shareholder value.

- The approach to internal control should be risk-based, including an evaluation of the likelihood and impact of risks becoming a reality (a number of organizations have in the past focused on control without regard to risk, for example solely through the use of a control questionnaire).

- Review procedures must cover business, operational, compliance, as well as financial risk.

- Risk assessment and internal control should be embedded in ongoing operations.

- The board or relevant board committee should receive relevant reports during the year on internal control and risk (many companies have previously followed only an annual review process for Cadbury compliance).

- The principal results of the group-wide risk identification, evaluation, and management review should be reported up to, and reviewed at, board level.

The real challenge is to build an effective and sound internal control and risk assessment process that is embedded within the business and monitored up to board level.

Corporate governance and risk management

A number of corporate failures – notably the collapses of BCCI and Polly Peck in the early 1990s in the UK – spurred on efforts to find an effective way of regulating board behaviour. In fact, corporate governance, as it came to be known, developed into a world-wide phenomenon, with many countries proposing reforms for effective corporate self-regulation.

The objective of corporate governance is to provide a blueprint for companies to manage in the interests of all stakeholders – not just the managers. It is a control system intended to provide a balance between managerial risk-taking and entrepreneurial energy with effective monitoring, so that management interests are aligned with the interests of those who have entrusted their capital to the enterprise and other stakeholders.

Corporate governance, in many ways, reflects legal reality. Company law guides that managers are required to manage the company's affairs in the best interests of the company – primarily shareholders. This is not to prevent risks from being taken. The reason for the development of the limited liability company, for example, was to encourage the assumption of risk in the furtherance of commercial endeavour.

Corporate governance also goes hand in hand with competition at the level of the global economy. The competition for resources in markets – financial, human or otherwise – dictates that they will be allocated where they will be most efficiently used. Good management compliments competition.

The 1992 report of the Cadbury Committee in the UK adopts the competition theory of corporate governance.

> 'The country's economy depends on the drive and efficiency of its companies. The effectiveness with which boards discharge their responsibilities determines [their] competitive position. They must be free to drive their companies forward, but exercise that freedom within the framework of effective accountability. That is the essence of any system of good corporate governance.'

Throughout the 1990s there has been an important convergence of risk management and corporate governance, including a convergence of internal audit and risk assessment. At the same time the definition of risk has been broadened out. At first, it meant a focus on internal controls, especially financial. Now, risk management under the corporate governance umbrella refers to 'all relevant risks' (see the Turnbull report). Companies are now obliged to consider the potential risks of environmentally unfriendly policies, corporate ethics, changes in the market, new technology, sexual harassment in the office, and so on.

The Combined Code on corporate governance (Turnbull Committee, 1999) will oblige companies to institutionalize risk assessment in their corporate cultures.[1] New auditing units may now report directly to the board rather than, say, the finance director.

The adoption of the Combined Code could positively impact companies' external image. Publicizing high standards of risk management could well confer competitive advantage. There are already signs of improved dialogue between shareholders and corporations that have adopted risk-based approaches to strategy and operations, and companies can reduce their cost of capital.

The Combined Code will draw the attention of the analyst community, making them look more closely at organizations' risk assessment procedures than has been the case in the past. According to the Association of Risk and Insurance Managers (AIRMIC), companies could become more entrepreneurial in their approach to business if they had better knowledge of all the risks involved and were consequently better able to cover them. This could enhance shareholder value. Firms that are able to demonstrate sound risk management procedures will become a more attractive prospect for investors, especially if the company operates in a volatile marketplace. As a result, risk management policy could become an important factor in an organization's market value in the future. Investors may feel more comfortable for organizations to embark on more risky ventures if management can demonstrate that risks to the business are understood and being managed.

[1]The Combined Code on Corporate Governance which sets out the final guidance on the implementation of the internal control requirements was published in 1999 by the Institute of Chartered Accountants in England and Wales. The guidance requires companies to identify, evaluate and manage their significant risks and to assess the effectiveness of the related internal control system. Boards of directors are called on to review regularly reports on the effectiveness of the system of internal control in managing key risks, and to undertake an annual assessment for the purpose of making their statements on internal control in the annual report. The guidance 'Internal Control: Guidance for Directors on the Combined Code' has the support and endorsement of the London Stock Exchange.

Conducting a baseline exercise

Management may carry out a baseline exercise to assess the current status of risk management practices across the organization. The scope of work may include examining:

- significant business, operational, financial and compliance risks;

- the potential financial and reputational impact and likelihood of those risks;

- the effectiveness of the management of those risks and the related internal control processes;

- necessary actions being taken to remedy any shortcomings or exploit opportunities more effectively; and

- potential improvements in monitoring of those risks (for example, those key performance indicators to be monitored by management or boards).

The output from this review is likely to be an action plan defining those tasks to be carried out to improve the existing risk management framework to an acceptable level. As part of this process, criteria for success should be defined and agreed.

Immediate action plan for the board and senior management

- Decide your stance – basic compliance or business improvement?
  - What are the wider benefits for the business?

- Evaluate your current status and plan for improvements using this tool:
  - What is the current status of risk management processes and the significance of any gaps?
  - What is the overall risk profile of the business?
  - What is the history of past control failures?

- Decide whether the board or a board committee will conduct the regular reviews required.

- Decide on timing in relation to transitional arrangements.

- Obtain approval for the proposed approach from the full board.

- Consider how to build and maintain momentum.

- Have you identified a board level sponsor?

- Do you need to set up a steering group?

- Have you identified a change manager or process owner?

- Do you have the necessary skills and time?

- Is there training needed?

- How do you incentivize the business to adopt any recommendations?

- Communicate and roll out to business managers – baseline exercise, ongoing reporting regime.

- Monitor progress against deadlines.

Building on the baseline

Organizations will need to agree on a process by which these criteria can be monitored and reported on at intervals during their next accounting period so that they can report that they have implemented an ongoing process. This could easily become a bureaucratic 'paper chase' if not carefully designed. Some approaches could include:

- cyclical reports from each business unit;

- monthly/quarterly exception reporting within existing divisional chief executive operating reports;

- brief risk update attached to monthly financial reports or quarterly re-forecasting;

- incorporation of risk and control within the annual business planning cycle and other key decision making processes; and

- a risk management database.

How ready is your organization?

The following questions aim to give board members a quick assessment of which areas of the guidance might prove most challenging for their organization and hence where most attention should be focused:

- Does risk management have top level sponsorship?

- Is risk management explicitly linked to business objectives and shareholder value?

- Has the board set appropriate objectives and policies on risk management and internal controls?

- Does the board have a clear idea of the high priority areas?

- Is there regular, robust reporting to the board on risk?

- What is the prevalent attitude towards risk management within the company?

- Could individual managers tell you what their key risk areas are and where improvements in risk management are most needed?

- Is there open and honest communication between management and the board on risk-related issues?

- Is risk management and internal control embedded throughout the business?

- Does the system of internal control contribute to implementing the policies adopted by the board?

- Does the business keep its system of internal control fresh and responsive to change?

References

The Turnbull Committee (1999) Internal Control: Guidance for Directors on the Combined Code. Institute of Chartered Accountants in England and Wales.

Further reading

Bradley, Stephen P. and Nolan, Richard L. (1998) *Sense and Respond –
Capturing Value in the Network Era*, Harvard Business School Press.

Bernstein, Peter L. (1996) *Against the Gods – The Remarkable Story of
Risk*, John Wiley & Sons Inc.

Beroggi, Giampiero E.G. and Wallace, William A. (1998) *Operational
Risk Management – The Integration of Decision, Communications
and Multimedia Technologies*, Kluwer Academic Publishers.

Cadbury Report (1992) Report of the Committee on The Financial
Aspects of Corporate Governance, Gee Publishing Ltd.

Chapman, C.B. and Ward, C.B. (1998) *Project Risk Management –
Processes, Insights and Techniques*, John Wiley and Sons.

Euromoney Books (1998) *The Practice of Risk Management*,
Euromoney Books.

Feldman, Mark L. and Spratt, Michael F. (1999) *Five Frogs on a Log*,
Harper Business.

Gamlen, Edwin and Phillips, John (1992) *Business Interruption
Insurance: Theory and Practice*, Buckley Press.

Gray, Jim and Reuter, Andreas (1993) *Transaction Processing:
Concepts and Techniques*, Morgan Kaufmann Publishers.

Greaver II, Maurice F. (1999) *Strategic Outsourcing,* AMACOM.

Greenbury Report (1995) Directors' Remuneration – A Report of a
Study Chaired by Sir Richard Greenbury, Gee Publishing Ltd.

Hammer, Michael and Champy, James (1993) *Reengineering the
Corporation – A Manifesto for Business Revolution*, Nicholas
Brealey Publishing.

Hampel Report (1998) The Committee on Corporate Governance, Gee
Publishing Ltd.

Henley, Ernest J. and Kumamoto, Hiromitsu (1999) *Probabilistic Risk
Assessment – Reliability Engineering, Design, and Analysis*, IEEE Press.

Johnson, Barry (1998) *Associates, joint ventures and other joint
arrangements*, Commercial Colour Press.

Johnson, Mike (1997) *Outsourcing – in brief*, Butterworth–Heinemann.

Kreitzman, Leon (1999) *The 24 Hour Society*, Profile Books.

Pantry, Sheila and Griffiths, Peter (1997) *The complete guide to preparing and implementing service level agreements,* Library Association Publishing.

Pendergrast, Mark (1999) *Uncommon Grounds*, Basic Books.

Peters, Glen (1996) *Beyond the Next Wave – Imagining the next generation of customers*, Pitman Publishing.

Pfister, Gregory F. (1998) *In Search of Clusters*, 2nd edition, Prentice Hall PTR.

Pradhan, Dhiraj K. (1996) *Fault-Tolerant Computer System Design*, Prentice Hall PTR.

Turnbull Committee (1999) Internal Control: Guidance for Directors on The Combined Code, The Institute of Chartered Accountants in England and Wales.

White, Robert and James, Barry (1996) *The Outsourcing Manual*, Gower Publishing.

Index